The Mechanics
of Golf

The Mechanics of Golf

by

ALEX HAY

Illustrated by the Author

ST. MARTIN'S PRESS
NEW YORK

ROBERT HALE
LONDON

© Alex Hay 1979

St. Martin's Press, Inc
175 Fifth Avenue
New York, N.Y. 10010

First published in the United
States of America 1979

Library of Congress Catalog
Card Number 79-64109

ISBN 0–312–52450–1

First published in Great Britain 1979

ISBN 0 7091 6090 9

Robert Hale Limited
Clerkenwell House
Clerkenwell Green
London, EC1

Photoset, printed and bound
in Great Britain by
REDWOOD BURN LIMITED
Trowbridge & Esher

Contents

5

1

The Golf Swing

The mystery which surrounds the golf swing is born entirely of misunderstanding. There is no secret. The golf swing is a logical chain of events. If it can be clearly understood then a balanced swing may be obtained by almost everyone. Of course there are individuals who, owing to some lack of physical co-ordination, will never swing a golf club correctly, but in the main most bad golfers swing that way simply, as I have stated, out of misunderstanding or misinterpretation. It is my intention in writing and illustrating this book to explain how the golf swing should work, in the hope that the combination of words and pictures may make understanding easier. It is not my intention to aim the knowledge gained over twenty-five years of learning, studying and teaching golf directly at beginners, although it would certainly be most suited to them. Rather, I hope that any golfer of any standard who feels a bit 'lost' may find help in these pages. I believe that the statement often made that a golf teacher may be good for beginners but no good for experienced players is absolute nonsense. He either understands how a swing works or he does not. If he is building a swing into a beginner then he must shape that person as well as the material will permit. Should he be making a simple adjustment to a good player then he must be able to make it causing the very minimum of disturbance to that person's mental picture of his swing. He can either teach or he cannot.

At present there are no teaching diplomas or certificates to prove that a person can teach golf, so until such awards come along, the best qualification must be experience. I, as fate would have it, gained my qualification in what has proved to be a most fortunate manner. I had endured a couple of years in the Stock Exchange in Edinburgh, not because of my great flair for finance, but because in those days, unlike today, it was almost the only business where one could be on the golf course at four o'clock and all day on Saturday. My introduction to the golf profession came when I joined the staff of Ben Sayers of North Berwick in 1950. My job there was twofold. During the winter months I was to learn the art of clubmaking, which by and large meant the buffing of those horrible groove-soled clubs on a machine which pitted my face around my safety goggles with a hideous green soap, and filing square handles on to the famous Benny putters. Then in the summer, armed with the knowledge I had gained I was put out to pasture on the famous links so that I might educate the rich English visitors, who funnily enough all seemed to be stockbrokers, into the rare science of a Scottish golf swing. The natural ability of the self-taught Scot was seemingly sufficient in the eyes of 'Old Ben', since his sole piece of advice in all the time I was with him was that if I tucked a handkerchief under the gentleman's right armpit and asked him to keep it there while he hit the ball, then although I would do him very little good, I could certainly do him very little harm. If it did happen to apply, then I might get a tip over and above the fee. Since Ben kept the fee and I relied on the tip, I prayed it would.

This valuable piece of information, which in fact was one of the most disastrous destroyers of width of arc and which I shall deal with later, was simply a means of flattening the plane of the swing. In those days we assumed that the Scots swung flat and the English upright, so it seemed the right thing to do at the time. In recent years my stockbroker has had revenge for his colleagues, as it certainly seems that I have heard that expression from him only too often. I do not mean the handkerchief under the arm, rather his, "I'm sorry, Alex, but it seemed the right thing to buy at the time".

One might wonder at my comment that I learned to teach golf in a fortunate manner, since the knowledge I gained at North Berwick would hardly seem much of a contribution. In fact this was not the case. It taught me just how little I knew; it taught me how I could be humbled by my inability to understand what I should really have been looking for, and when I met a man who really knew his subject I soaked him up like blotting paper out of sheer appreciation. I joined the staff of Bill Shankland at Potters Bar Golf Club to continue my training. The days of the buffing machine and the square handles were over. I would think that Bill Shankland has, with the exception of Tony Jacklin, turned out from his apprentices very few competitive players. He has produced good club professionals and good teachers. This is not uncommon; when one studies the history of our well-known teachers one finds very few good players coming through from their stable. This is simply because they delve so deep into the science of the swing that their students become such Thinkers that they, in the end are *reduced* to becoming Teachers. A strange comment, but true. What then, you may ask, happened to Jacklin? Well, 'the Boss' never really got through to him. Tony was of the material which makes players, not teachers, or club professionals; the hardened crust which has to surround players could only be penetrated to a depth which he allowed. He had no interest whatsoever in being a teacher. So in a sense Shankland's greatest failure was his greatest success.

On the other hand I, who really wanted to learn, who appreciated how embarrassing it was to be sent out unarmed, found myself with one of the finest teachers in the game, who passed on willingly all the knowledge I could absorb. His insistence was that many teachers were not good enough, not because they did not know but because they did not know how to explain. "GOLF NEEDS CLARIFICATION," he would roar, thumping his great fist down with each syllable. On that statement I have tried to base all of my teaching, and I am so pleased at the end of a lesson if a pupil claims that he has never 'seen' it so clearly ever before, or that for the first time he has really understood what he was trying to do. When I was on a recent golfing trip to America I picked up a small plaque in Disneyland which I feel applies so well to teaching golf. It states:

I know you believe you understand what you think I said, but I am not sure you realize that what you heard is not what I meant.

I brought it home with me intending to hang it in my shop but my wife thought it applied to my behaviour at home, so it hangs in the kitchen.

The only other man I have worked with who can *clarify* as Shankland did is Sid Collins, head instructor at our P.G.A. Training School for Assistants. It is fantastic being on his panel of instructors just to watch him at work. Young assistants who thought they knew it all cannot believe the simplicity with which he interprets the golf swing. He does more for some of their swings in five minutes than has been done so far in their careers. He clarifies so beautifully that past complications just melt away. I am pleased that Sid vetted most of the material in this book and that it agrees with what he has been teaching for years. It is a great pity that other teachers could not have recognized the way the golf swing had to go, as he did.

I spent a few years as club professional to the East Herts Club teaching, as one does at a private club, a variety of pupils, from complete beginners to experienced players, from children to the aged and infirm, the ones the doctors send along when all else has passed them by. Then fate took a hand and I took a step which, unfortunately, not every teacher can experience, since it is the way to become as complete a teacher as possible. I joined a brand new club, Dunham Forest in Cheshire, begun by a nucleus of about twenty-five established players who, when I finished some five years later, had grown to two hundred full-playing members. This is the education of all time. This has to be the finishing school for any golf teacher. An average club professional in these days of three- and four-year waiting lists for membership will probably deal with no more than a dozen or so beginners in a year. I was introduced, in a haze of champagne, on the club's opening day to some two hundred and taught them all! Seeing so many people of all ages, shapes and sizes, I could not help but find the easiest ways of conveying to them in the simplest of terms what was necessary to make a swing. I found that after months spent with such a volume of beginners I was devising methods of explaining so that they could pick up my meaning the first time. Beginner golfers are a soul-destroying breed and explaining a point several times to one is frustrating enough but to two hundred it would surely produce insanity. Tough as it was it carried me on from Shankland's insight and ability to make clear, and proved to me his words "Golf needs clarification".

Thanks to the well-known BBC Golf Correspondent Tom Scott I was made able, through the medium of his magazine *Golf Illustrated*, not only to expound on the mechanics of the golf swing as I see them, but was given the opportunity to illustrate, which is something I have longed to do. When Ben Hogan wrote his famous book and had it illustrated by Ravielli it was brought home that drawings are a better medium than photographs for instruction. In golf in particular, which is a game of tremendous 'feel', a photograph can be a dangerous item, since it shows what is actually happening and not what a teacher may wish his pupil to feel is happening. I have personally never taught by the use of videotape because, whilst I believe that it might well be advantageous to the very good player with only a slight flaw, it could be heartbreaking to a high handicapped, poorer player, where a teacher may have had to add a patch to a deformed swing. The pupil, doing what he has been told to feel, and doing it well, may be hitting the ball very well, but in fact if he saw himself he would be destroyed. So sometimes it has to be "feel what I want you to feel and believe it looks good". Perhaps then with an artist's eye for anatomy and movement plus the enjoyment derived from making people improve through a better understanding, I feel sufficiently trained and experienced to explain the mechanics of the golf swing in this book.

The golf swing has often been mistakenly described as an un-natural movement, but this is only because it cannot be mastered without guidance and without it should not be attempted. Leave a man with a golf club and some balls and within minutes, with the aid of natural talent, he would be shaping himself almost certainly towards a disastrous golfing future. He would certainly not arrive at the grip which he must master if consistency is ever to be achieved. By gripping in the manner most comfortable he would, with only a few minutes of application, and providing the club he was using was a lofted iron, be hitting the ball into the air with little difficulty. Left to his own resources for a month or two he would be virtually incurable. Many would argue that there are good players who have not had a golf lesson in their lives but I do not believe this. There is, besides instruction from a skilled teacher, instruction by copying. The good player who has had no direct tuition must therefore be a good copier.

Beginning golf properly is a tedious affair since in fact the golf swing must be learned backwards. By that I mean that the ingredient which enables the player to hit the ball is the per-fectly natural feel of the hands whipping the clubhead, by means of the shaft. But before this luxury of nature may take place, (and it is natural, being the same sort of talent that makes a person able to bounce a stone across water or whip the top off a dandelion with a stick, except that it is done with two hands), a platform must be built in order that the swinger may consistently hit the ball vast distances. This platform we call the orthodox swing, and to achieve the very best of results all of the golfing departments of the body must contribute. Imagine, if you will, two identical twins, exactly alike in every detail. Give one a club and some balls and send him off for a few weeks on his own. Take the other and without allowing him the luxury of feel or natural flair teach him the positions from which he will surely achieve his best results in the future. Bring them together and the pupil will wonder why he has been wasting his time and his money. His twin will be hitting the ball with apparent ease every time, whilst he is still struggling with routine movements. However, by the time some six months have gone by and the pupil is beginning to see daylight with a little of his natural talent attaching itself to his method, we would find the twin already at his peak, with very little more to come. By the time a year had passed the untaught twin would have shaped himself around a grip of comfort, allowing his natural flair to design his arc, but unfortunately for him his mould would be well on the way to a disastrous setting. On the other hand, the pupil, correctly taught, would have for himself a future determined only by his natural aptitude, dedication and time available. So this is why the game is, as I have said, often described as unnatural. In my opinion it is completely natural – after certain precautions have been taken.

Obviously there are many occasions where a student realizes the danger and does not take advice, but studies every article printed and attempts to involve every theory. As a result he paralyses any natural talent which he may possess. Every golf club has at least one such individual. He is to be found standing on the first tee completely locked up, performing some sort of countdown, until he is like the centipede who was asked which foot he led off with. Paralysis by analysis! We used to have one such person at Potters Bar who took in every word, written or otherwise, and who had as his main fault a tendency to close the face of the club. The cause was that he simply turned his left hand too far over the handle when taking up his hold on the club. He decided that the best cure would be to write the correct instructions on a card which he stuck on to the back of his glove so that he could read the information just prior to starting his swing. There was no doubt that this helped him and he set off in his Sunday fourball with a cracking drive. When he arrived back in the pro shop we only had to look at his face to see that it had not lasted. The reason? During the first few holes he had picked up so many tips from his cronies that he had decided to add them to his list. By the time he had read down to No. 6 his hand was farther over than ever!

It would be extremely rash, even stupid to say that the golf swing is a simple thing. No one in his right mind would ever claim that, especially someone who has lived with it day in and day out. But understanding it is not so difficult. Curing its faults, and adjusting and balancing a swing so that a player might return to lost form or improve his game, is not difficult either, provided one understands just how the swing is made up. Like an engine there are several components, all of which must be understood so that they may be balanced or tuned to work smoothly together and perform consistently. A player with knowledge of these components may deliberately unbalance them by leaving one out, and then by increasing another create a certain type of shot. When an experienced golfer arrives for some help because of loss of form, the teacher merely searches through a sequence to find which part is underfunctioning and which has increased in order to compensate. By rebalancing these he can bring the swing back into the shape which the player recognizes as his old familiar action. Most good teachers I have spoken to will diagnose the trouble in not more than two or three strokes, even with a complete stranger. The experienced eye, confirmed by the flight of the ball, is enough, and the necessary rebalancing may begin. Admittedly with the better player it is often more difficult to spot the trouble. With a beginner or a high handicap player, the problem usually sticks out like a sore thumb.

I have illustrated in this book the components of the swing in their correct sequence; showing how they contribute to the full swing so that the club may move round the player's body in a consistent circle, all the departments combining to create *feel, balanced acceleration* and *consistency* with all living under the protection of good *arc*.

The best way I can possibly describe a golf swing is by comparing it with a parcel. Think of the packaging as the arc. It is very necessary to protect the important items contained within, and if the wrapping is loose and untidy then the parcel may never arrive. If it is neat and well presented then it will get to its destination without difficulty. What the packaging is protecting is also important, in this case it is the swing's *hand action*.

15

Imagine how you would feel if a beautifully wrapped package arrived and inside was nothing. The whole operation would be pointless. Equally pointless on the other hand would be some valuable item tossed about without the protection of a proper package. The golf swing is a hand action hidden within an arc. The hand action uses the arc as a platform from which it may deliver the acceleration of the clubhead safely and smoothly through the ball. Many great players swing their arc so beautifully, so smoothly, that the acceleration by the hands blends and goes unseen by the layman's eyes, who later attempts to follow his misguided impression of the great player until his hand work deteriorates completely and all feel is lost. The self-taught creature may be easily recognized since he sets off immediately using the flair and the feel of his hand action without the protection of a proper package, the platform we call the arc. Without this protection he is lost.

2

The Sequence

The pages of this book are deliberately written in a *sequence*. This is not only the key to learning about the swing but the formula which teachers go through in search of a swing fault. Finding a fault in a swing is not spotting the obvious. Any idiot can do that, and there are always plenty of those around to give 'friendly advice'. The clever part is not just spotting the fault but spotting the source. It is only at the source that the trouble can be cleared permanently. Teachers of great experience use the same sequence, many of them no doubt unaware that they do it, but it is the case.

The sequence is there as a guide in the building of a good golf swing and it is there to help trace and cure a fault. To search for a fault without proper regard for the sequence would be futile, for the obvious fault is most certainly created by a mistake at an earlier stage. The sequence is:

GRIP   BLADE   BALL POSITION   STANCE   POSTURE
SET-UP   BACKSWING   DOWNSWING   THROUGHSWING
FOLLOW-THROUGH

To search for the cure of a closing clubface at the impact, for example, without having checked the GRIP would be insanity. To criticize an overswing without examining the POSTURE or the SET-UP would be stupid. For a teacher to tolerate a pupil's request to cure a fault, but with the proviso "do not touch my bad grip because it is uncomfortable to change it", is unthinkable. There is no excuse for neglect of the early parts of the sequence, the ones which happen before the swing proper begins. GRIP, BALL POSITION, STANCE, POSTURE all take the player to the launching pad of correct movement, the SET-UP. The expression is self-descriptive, a player shapes his swing from it and back through it.

17

1 POSITIVE THINKING

It is absolutely essential that the whole mental approach to learning, to curing, and to using the golf swing must be POSITIVE. Any experienced player who is curing a fault by saying to himself whilst he is swinging, "I must not do this" has no chance. He must know what he has got to do and say "I am doing it". A good example is overswinging on the backswing. The difference between shortening the swing by thinking "I must not go so far back" and by thinking "I must be fully prepared in a shorter distance" is critical. The first is the player telling himself to make do with something less than he has up till then felt necessary and this will show in the authority of the stroke.

Spectators wonder at the firmness top players put into their short pitch shots. This happens because the expert treats the smaller stroke as a stroke in its own right, one deserving a positive strike. The average club player thinks of a short shot as a cut-down of his full one. He uses the negative "I must not hit it too hard".

I have deliberately sequenced these pages in a positive form to help a beginner compile a swing and to help more experienced players understand better the mechanics of the swing so that they may check for faults in the correct order. To find the obvious is simple, but the danger of attempting to cure a flaw without tracing its source, without back-tracking through the sequence to the origin, lends itself to curing by negative thinking. There would be little point in a player being aware that he is closing the face of the club at the top of the swing and trying to fix it by thinking that he "must not", before he has checked back to see that his GRIP is not the cause. If it is, then he may take positive steps to repair the fault.

2 THE THREE CHECKPOINTS

An early detection of trouble is essential, for the milder the treatment required for a cure the better, since any one department demanding strong concentration will be given it at the expense of the others. The brain can only focus on one part and that part should be the complete shape of the swing, compiled into a pattern of muscular movements memorized by continual repetition. It may make mild adjustments, have mild awareness of positions, but it cannot stand a total commitment to any one part. Often tournament players are heard to say that they concentrated for a whole round on a hunch they had on the practice ground prior to teeing off. This is the added comfort of an extra positive thought which they adopt into their overall shape of swing. For a beginner it is best that he concentrates his thinking on three positive points in the swing: THE SET-UP, THE TOP OF THE BACKSWING, and THE FOLLOW-THROUGH.

A correct SET-UP provided a framework for the movements to come. The TOP OF THE BACKSWING shows him that he is correctly poised, balanced and in PLANE to get maximum PULL back through the ball. The FOLLOW-THROUGH is there to prove that all that went into the other two was correct, and that it resulted in complete balance and position.

Each of the three should be done separately, without a ball, holding each for a second or two to establish them, for they will become the OVERALL SWING SHAPE when they join together. The muscular pattern will follow, the time gap between each position will reduce and the three POSITIVE POSITIONS blend into one.

3 THE CORRECT PRIORITY OF HAND ACTION

I have stated that hand action is essential to good swinging but it will become apparent to readers that I feel very much aware that excessive, or independent, hand action is one of the most unnecessary and dangerous factors in the game. Too much is more harmful than not enough. Hand action is something we are either born with or we are not and all sorts of weird cranking exercises are going to do no good to someone who has not got natural flair. Without that flair, a person would be better without any conscious hand work, using the arc to gain consistency rather than flapping about trying to create that which he cannot.

I remember as a child in Scotland our hobby was whipping a top, or as we called it, a peerie. Another was bouncing flat stones across the Firth of Forth. The kids who could never keep the peerie spinning were also the ones who saw their stones disappear in a single plop. They had not got the natural flair. When we reached the ripe old age of ten or so and took to golf, it was the same few who were backward again.

The beauty of the modern golf swing is that good hand action is not the difficult unrolling of the wrists that it used to be. The modern golf club design has placed fewer demands on the player, and the need for flair and timing that was essential is a

19

much simpler-to-find skill. From old-style golf clubs which by their design led to a rolling of the wrists, to the finely balanced instruments of today a better, more easily acquired hand action has evolved. By placing the hands on the handle correctly, the wrist joints are so positioned that the natural movements created when the arc is in motion makes adequate hand action occur. It is also sheltered in the protection of a plane so that a consistently angled circle is created around the player's body. I repeat that hand action is essential. The man with the good hands will be the best player, but the method of swinging the club I have written about and illustrated in this book would eliminate the dangers which a man with good hands would fall into if he persists in using those hands as the be-all and end-all of the swing. For the player with the 'not so good hands', if he applies the same he would certainly do better than to flap about hingeing and flicking to try and locate something he cannot. Swinging in direct plane with the hands and clubface remaining square to that plane is safety for all. The only exception is the person who, either by age or by disability, cannot turn the body sufficiently, and who then has to run the risk of extra wrist movement with the complicated timing which that involves. A wristy swing is a good way to swing the club if it is the only way left to achieve the pleasure of golf, but it is a compromise. To see young people with good hands taking on the risks of rolling the clubface, arguing with the correct plane for their physique, is quite tragic.

The Americans recognized the dangers sooner, but we in Britain, perhaps with our leanings to tradition, stayed with the rolling-the-club method, admiring those with flair whilst suffering the indignity of slicing if we did not have it. The only cure offered for the slice seemed to be to show more knuckles on the left hand. Many frustrated slicers must have wondered at the Americans who came over here with one knuckle showing and hitting the ball with a draw. They had recognized that the left hand could hinge at the wrist joint and still have the back of the left hand, the back of the left arm, and the clubface all in parallel, all tilted on the correct plane angle. When the downswing started, there was no need for a difficult-to-time repair job to get back to the ball. The return journey was natural and simple.

Even though the top American players were evolving the swing as we see it today in almost all of them, it is not yet clarified by

20

the people who write about it. A complete book recently devoted its pages to the square method, to make it all clear to the golfing public. A follow-up has since been released with an explanation that in the first version, "Some of its principles were misinterpreted by both teachers and weekend players and some of the positions it called for were difficult to attain".

The original showed positions which it claimed to be correct "although very few professionals could actually do them". This of course was not because the professional could not do them but because they were wrong!

The players are the correct ones, for they have to pay dearly for inaccuracy and it is their need for correct movement under pressure which has brought the square-to-the-plane swing about. It is not their fault that it has proved the most controversial and that it cannot be interpreted or clarified.

I have illustrated the square-to-the-plane swing in these pages so that it may be understood to the great advantage of golfers. The positions I describe are not my idea, nor do I claim to have discovered a method. Nobody discovers methods in golf – they evolve. The principles in this book are those used by the great majority of the world's greatest, written and drawn so that we all may understand them.

3

The Grip

Some years ago I took part in a golf clinic, being one of a panel of four golf professionals. A member of the audience asked about the importance of a good grip. The 'expert' who chose to answer the question was at the time one of the country's top players. He was a tournament winner on several occasions and I was absolutely astonished when he said that how one gripped the club did not matter. So long as the hands were close together and the golfer had a good feel of the club that would be sufficient. He could not have been farther from the truth. The whole success or failure of a golf swing stems from the way the club is held. The position of the hands on the handle determines the way the wrists may be permitted to hinge. The angle of tilt, or in other words the plane of the swing, would certainly be misguided completely from a poor grip. It is the feel that may be created when the two hands are together properly that joins the package of the swing as I have described it. They are the link-up between the solid building of the arc and the sparkling flair of feel. It is absolutely necessary that the hands should be placed properly on the handle so that they may, opposites though they are, work as a unit in their huge contribution to making the swing.

In order that this can happen, the first thing that has to be accepted is that the palms must be parallel, for if one palm is turned at an angle from the other then the bone structure of the forearms would be in argument. When these two arms are travelling at high speed through the ball they must agree which should be upright. By upright I mean that if the arms hang by the side of the body and are swung directly upwards, the palms of the hands are facing each other and the two bones which make up each forearm are one above the other. It is essential that these two sets of bones travel throughout the swing as near

to parallel as is humanly possible. Should they set off, by means of a bad grip, out of line then they are going not only to perform in a deforming manner throughout the swing, making a simple arc an impossibility, but when they arrive back in the area where the ball is to be hit they will both, by nature's requirements, be trying to find upright. The battle will be on, and it is a battle in which there are no winners. Only when the grip is taken up with the palms parallel can the two pairs of bones be allowed true parallel movement through the swing and through the strike. The grip is therefore the very essence of consistency.

1 LEFT HAND

There can be little doubt that learning to grip the club is a most painful experience for golf's beginners. In fact, the advice a teacher feels inclined to give to a first-day pupil is that should the hands feel at all comfortable, the grip is wrong! Even experienced players who have slipped into an incorrect hold refuse to believe that they were ever taught the correct one. However, the fact remains that with a bad grip it is 99 per cent certain that bad golf will follow and although a good grip will not guarantee good golf, it certainly makes it possible. It is necessary that a pupil, beginner or experienced, understands not only how but why he has to grip in the correct manner.

The handle must be placed, *after the arm has reached slightly outwards and the fingers are pointed to the turf,* across the left hand at an angle almost parallel to the line of the arm. It is secured at its top end into the seam which divides the palm from the callus pad and it leaves the hand resting on the forefinger tip.

The shaft becomes almost a continuation of the arm and the strength of bringing the end three fingers upwards and the heel of the hand downwards engages the muscles down the back of the forearm. I refer to muscles without implying there has to be great strength, but there must be a consistency of pressure. It is quite amazing how many golfers allow the handle to slip over the heel of the palm and in fact secure the club only by the thumb joint, disconnecting the back muscles of the forearm from the grip.

Whilst the forward part of the hand contributes little to the actual strength of the hold through the action of the swing, it is the part the player relies on for a constant relationship between his hand, the back of his forearm, and the clubface.

It is essential that if the clubface is to strike consistently square through the ball, the back of the left hand must work with it. The correct left-hand position when viewed by the player looking directly down on hand and clubface is one which shows two knuckle joints. The easiest way of providing the two knuckles is to place the thumb a quarter of an inch to the right side of the handle, then to imagine that an instant adhesive has connected the palm side of the forefinger knuckle joint to the inside of the thumb.

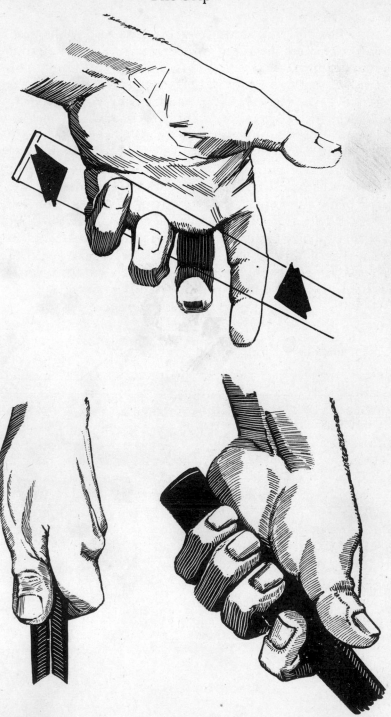

25

2 INTRODUCTION OF THE RIGHT HAND

Before knowing how to apply the right hand a player should realize just what the purpose of the hand is, for although the left hand and the right are very close together and in fact are virtually entwined, the roles of the two hands are just that bit different. Where the left is very much involved with the support and strength of the arc the right is there to create feel, suppleness and precision. For these reasons the handle of the club must lie across the fingers of the right hand as I have illustrated.

Imagine if you would placing a golf ball in the centre of the palm of the right hand and attempting to throw it for both distance and accuracy. Then compare how different it would feel if the ball were placed in the fingers of the hand. Suddenly the wrist would become free and supple. I am not for a minute suggesting that golf is a wristy flick, but one must realize that

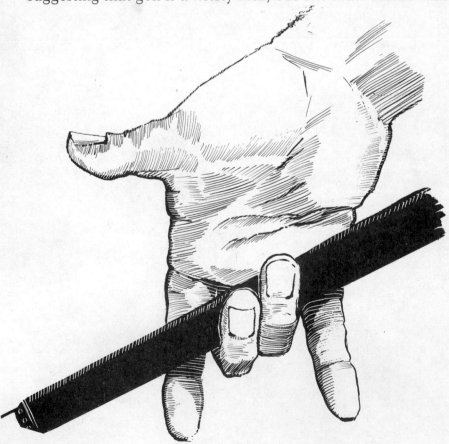

when the swing builds up its leverage to the top of the back-swing the shaft of the club will be at very least 90 degrees to the line of the left arm and at this stage the right wrist will be hinged at a very acute angle. Therefore it is a must for a supple-ness in that wrist joint which is not necessary in the left. For this reason alone a player must recognize the difference be-tween left-hand palm and finger grip and right-hand finger grip.

In my drawing I have shown the two centre fingers securing the handle and they almost entirely represent the strength of the right-hand grip. The extended little finger will overlap onto the forefinger of the left hand. The forefinger and thumb will come down onto the handle, thumb slightly to the left of the grip, forefinger to the right pinching the grip lightly and giving the feeling of precision and at the same time fitting snugly over the thumb of the left hand.

3 SECOND STAGE OF RIGHT HAND

The joining together of the right hand to the left is where great care must be taken. The Vardon Grip, which is the one I teach and the one surely taught by 99 per cent of golf instructors, is perfectly worked out so that both hands may perform their particular roles and yet complement the efforts of the other.

The left hand is well established on the handle, as it is the connection between arm and shaft. It has created, by the way it has secured the club, a unit which starts up in the left shoulder joint and ends up at the sole-plate of the club. In other words they are now one. The right hand is taking its place on the handle without disturbing this authority but preserving the right to function in a more supple manner, with its emphasis on feel and creative ability.

The centre two fingers have secured the main hold, and the little finger is shown doing all it has to, fitting over the forefinger of the left hand. Many people prefer to hook this little finger around behind the forefinger as though to derive more strength. This is not necessary, for the point of overlapping is mainly to keep the hands together so that although they have separate roles, they blend and lose their complete individuality which would be disastrous in a golf swing. They are going to work separately together!

From the drawing it will be seen that the finger grip of the right hand leaves available the soft under-palm beneath the right thumb so that this may settle down over the thumb of the left hand, completely hiding it from view, but at the same time steadying it onto the handle. The left thumb in return helps by filling up this cavity which a finger grip creates in the palm of the right hand.

It is this initial introduction of position that is so important. The final setting down of the forefinger and thumb of the right is so simple if care is shown at this stage.

The Grip

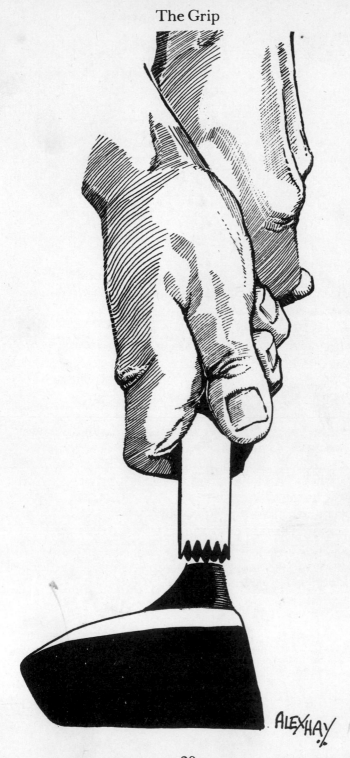

ALEX HAY

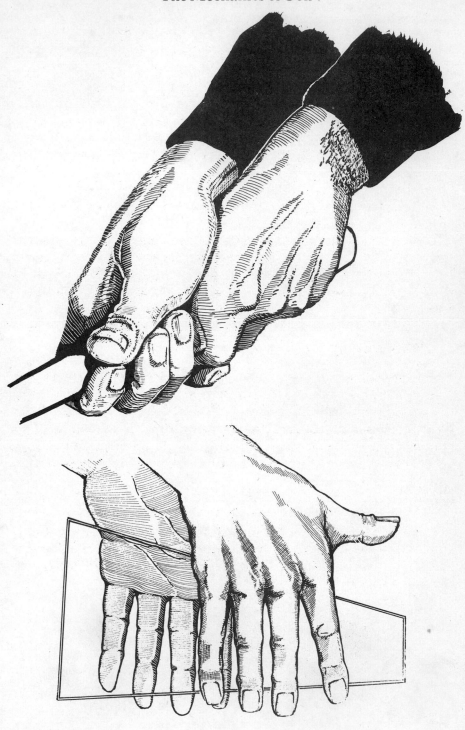

4 THE SHAPE OF THE GRIP

The final sealing down of the forefinger and thumb of the right hand leaves us with the perfect grip for golf, the Vardon Grip completed. Support at one end and flexibility at the other. And yet by the correct link-up in the centre there will be no need ever to feel "the left hand does this and the right hand does that".

The question often crops up as to why the handle of a golf club should be thicker at the top than at the bottom. Why should it not be parallel or even thinner at the top end, as one misguided manufacturer tried to do a few years ago, based on the theory that the little finger of the left hand was too small to get around the thickest part of the club.

There is good reason for its design. I have illustrated the wedge shape of good gripping of this two-handed game, covering the gripping areas of the two hands. The widest part involves not just the little finger of the left hand but an area which extends up the palm to above the callus pad. When this whole area enfolds the handle, a stability is brought into the wrist in order to support the golfing arc.

By the time the wedge shape has passed to the extremity at the other end it is only involved with the sensitive forefinger. So the wedge demonstrates the ultimate beauty of the correct hold, tapering from authority at one end in an angle through the two hands to the final accuracy at the other. And, as shown in the drawing, the little finger of the right hand is in position to slip over the forefinger of the left and bind the pair together in harmony.

In the case of a beginner the understanding of the grip would now be sufficient for him to embark on the building of an arc. Whilst he still has no idea of hand action his grip is in such a position that it will do no damage to the arc to be learned, and his wrists are positioned so that they may hinge naturally when required.

5 TOP OF SWING POSITION OF HANDS

I have illustrated the hands at the point where it is apparent whether the player has or has not taken up a correct hold of the club – the top of the backswing. Although it is accepted that the impact is where it all matters, this often leads to an idleness in a player's devotion to correct gripping, with him claiming that it does not matter how he grips the club so long as he gets the clubface square at the strike, and then holding the club in such a way that it is the exception rather than the rule that he strikes correctly. At the top of the swing, a position should be found which makes the downswing path almost a simple reversal of the upswing and certainly not a remedial action.

Holding the club as I have explained, with the left hand adopting a palm and finger grip and the right hand entirely finger, maintains the stability which joins the left forearm to the handle, allowing the plane or, in simple language, the angle of the swing to remain direct towards the ball, while the more supple right hand is encouraged to hinge to create the feel and the acceleration necessary in a good action.

In the modern golf swing used by most of the world's top competitors, the left wrist hinges as shown in the main drawing and yet maintains a direct line down the back of the hand and forearm (shown by the black line in the smaller drawing). The right hand has to hinge back on itself and condescends to be guided by the stability of the left, and yet because it is correctly placed on the handle it is still being prepared for what it has to do through the ball.

These hands are in the correct position, but I wish to describe some of the typical faults found in the grips of many players and to explain the variations of golf shots which may be created by each. In this way a reader may be able to associate himself with a type of stroke and so look to his grip.

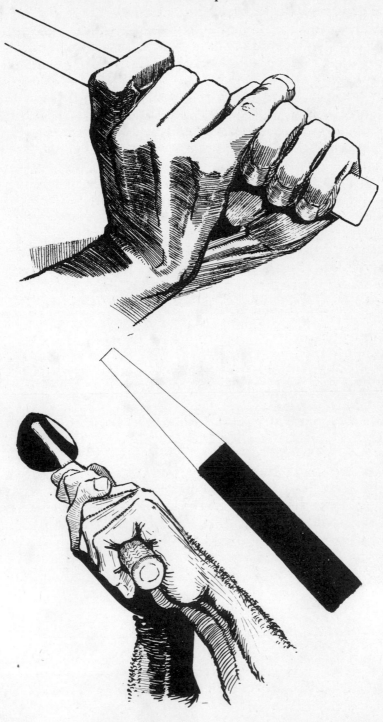

6 STRONG RIGHT HAND

There must be no argument in the direction that each hand is prepared to work in. This of course must happen if the palms of the hands are not parallel when the grip is taken up. Should the left hand take the handle so that the player can look directly down and see two knuckle joints, then the 'V' between the thumb and forefinger will point just to the right of his face. This has made the outside of the left forearm a parallel with the face of the club, both square to the target. But if he adds his right hand to the handle with its 'V' pointing more to his right, he creates an argument. At the stage in the backswing when the wrists have to cock, the out-of-line right hand has to get into a

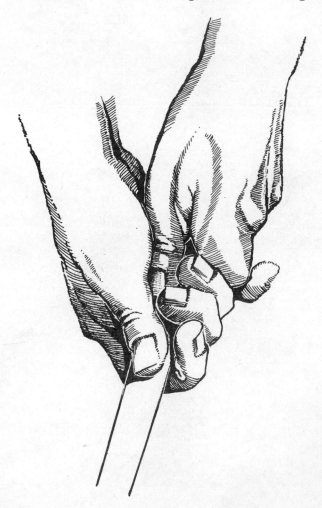

position from where it can hit the ball and being out of alignment it will almost certainly twist the left hand, and with it the clubface, out of square.

It is essential that the forefinger and thumb of the right hand look to their most important responsibility, their regard for position. The handle must be secured between the crook of the forefinger and the inside pad of the thumb, forming the 'V' shape as illustrated, over the handle. This action lightly squeezes thumb against forefinger knuckle joint, as happened in the left hand, and the line formed between the two should point just right of the player's face as he looks down.

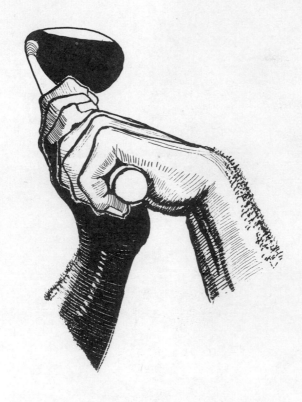

7 WEAK LEFT HAND

Although this grip fault is known as 'weak' the trouble with it is that it is not content to stay weak. The left hand, illustrated without the right hand obscuring, is on the handle in a position where, were the player to look directly downwards without leaning his head, he would count less than the minimum requirement of two knuckle joints. This is the weak grip, but immediately the swing commences, the hand and forearm assert themselves by means of a rotating movement so that they may

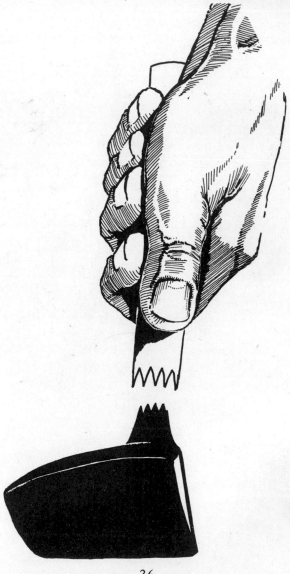

enjoy the feeling of strength which good position would have produced.

What happens to the clubhead is made clear in the illustration. It rolls open. But it rolls open into a strong position which it is very reluctant to give up. It much prefers to maintain the new-found strength and returns to the ball as it is. The clubface would then be many degrees to the right of the target, sending the ball off with sidespin. Many players who fall into this grip see the ball fly to the right and try to bring the ball back straight by heaving the shoulders. This only creates a swing across the ball and even more slice sidespin. This grip fault often arises simply from a lazy left side of the body, a subject which shall be enlarged upon in the chapter on Set-up. In many cases a player who has been criticized for having too strong a right hand and

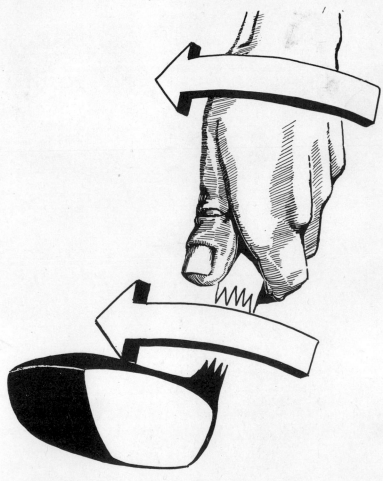

has taken action to get the right more on top has conveniently moved his left hand aside.

8 BOTH HANDS FALLING AWAY

Should a player fall into the trap where both hands have fallen away in an outwardly direction, he really has no hope whatsoever of making a golf swing. This is generally a fault of the complete novice. Experienced golfers may have one hand or the other in a weak position but it is unusual to find one with both weak.

There is no way that both hands can get through the whole action without one taking the initiative and attempting to get into a 'strong' position. This will cause an instant rebellion of the other.

The Grip

On the backswing, should the left rotate to find the strength of the orthodox two knuckles, the rotation would drive into the right forearm and elbow, forcing them to overthrow in the opposite rotation on the downswing.

Should the right hand try to show its strength in the backswing, the left wrist would be forced to arch outwards, putting any thoughts of good hand action through the ball out of the question.

In order to live with this situation the bending of both elbows is the only way that a swing can be created, and when elbows splay outwards, the building of a good swing is impossible.

Attention to other parts of the swing is what distracts a beginner's concentration from his hands, and the grip always

falls apart from neglect. The impression a novice should have is
that the hands are turned gently towards each other.

9 SHORT THUMB AND LONG THUMB

The incorrect placing of the handle across the left hand is done
for two reasons. One is for comfort and the other is to create a
feeling of greater strength in the weaker hand. Fortunately
there are give-away signs that may be checked quite easily and
remedial action taken.

Short thumb.   For greater comfort a player will place the handle
through the palm at too much of a slant. The pitfall is that the
club, throughout the swing, is held in place by the strength of
the thumb only and the left thumb is not designed for the job.
Comfort there might be, but good hand action there certainly
will not be. The tell-tale sign is that a position known as short
thumb will be seen when the player looks down on his hand.

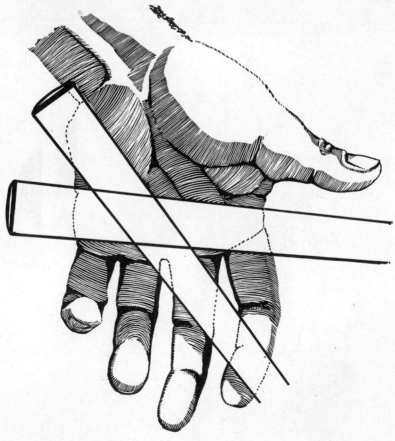

The forefinger will be extended further down the handle than the end of the thumb.

Long thumb. The grip taken up by a player seeking greater strength in his hold will be that he places the handle across the base of the palm at right angles to the fingers. The feeling of curling the fingers upwards gives a false illusion of great strength but unfortunately his wrist will have to arch unnaturally so that he may address the ball. This movement is extremely difficult to retrace during the swing and very inconsistent direction will be the result.

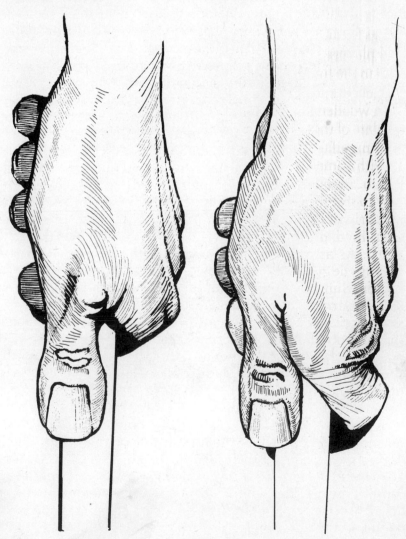

4

Blade

When a full understanding of the grip has been gained, the time has come to introduce the head of the club to the ball, to place the ball opposite the feet and to aim at the target. That sounds very simple but in fact great care must be taken so that the position of the ball and the width of the stance relate to the type of stroke to be played.

There is no difference in the placing behind the ball of the club-head, as far as alignment is concerned, for beginners or experienced players. The leading edge of the club must be at right angles to the intended line of flight of the ball. The only uncertainty occurs in judging just which edge is the leading one. With a wooden club very little difficulty is experienced, for the base plate of the club, being flat, will rest on the turf and if correctly manufactured, which unfortunately is not always the case with some so-called clubmakers, will present the face of the club directly at the target. It is of advantage to a golfer lightly to rest the base of the wood on the ground before taking up his grip of the club. There is not much point in securing a proper hold only to look down and find the clubhead is crooked. As association should be formed with the left hand taking up the grip and the even resting of the base of the club.

The iron club poses a different problem. Most conventional iron heads are fan shaped, broader at the toe than at the heel and many players fail to recognize that the angle of loft on the iron is set from the bottom edge upwards. It is therefore of great importance that the bottom edge is square to the target.

A very common mistake is often committed by golfers who have set their hands forward of the ball when intending to keep its flight low, perhaps when playing into a strong wind. Their hands go forward and the blade of the club turns open. The ball, instead of being driven low and forwards as was intended, is pushed away to the right.

In whichever direction the shaft may have to lean, the leading edge must stay right-angled to the target.

42

Blade

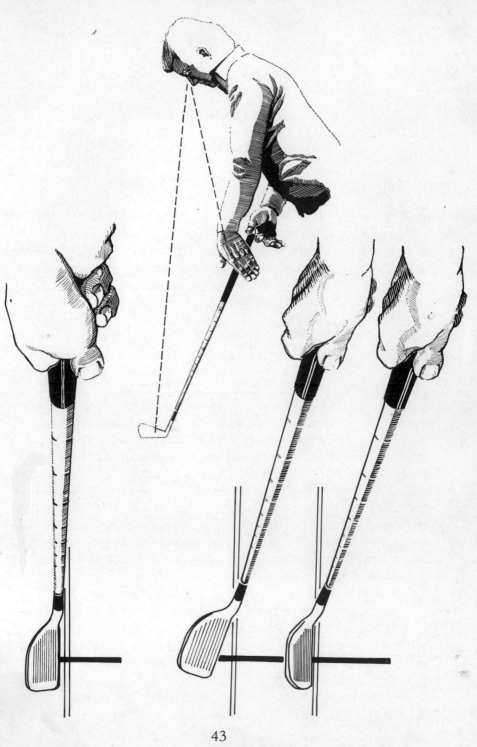

5

Ball Position

1 BEGINNERS
A beginner would be concerned with three basic ball positions which are matched up with three widths of stance and three strokes.

1. *Wooden clubs.* Owing to the fact that greater swing is required, more support and foundation are necessary so that the stance is at its widest. Approximately the width of the shoulders should be between the feet. Because of the considerable length of the club, the arc to be created must be shallow and will have a sweeping effect. Therefore the ball position is forward, opposite a point approximately one to two inches inside the left heel. This ball position will be the same for all wooden club strokes until progress is made when the ball shall be moved to a spot just inside the left heel for the driver.

2. *Middle irons.* Although these clubs will be swung quite powerfully the shorter shafts limit the amount of swing, and this will quite correctly narrow the arc. The feet will not be taking on the same load and so a slightly narrower stance than with the wood will be necessary. As a rule there is no tee peg under the ball as with wooden club strokes, and the ball is going to be squeezed from the turf rather than swept, so the ball is brought back to a spot just forward of centre.

3. *Short irons.* These are played for precision in an area where it is accuracy rather than power which matters, a narrower stance being then encouraged. In fact, on some very small strokes, many players benefit from the feet being very close together. This has the effect of making the player more aware of the feel of the clubhead. The lack of momentum in the swing requires the ball to be placed opposite the centre of the feet.

Ball Position

There is a danger for beginners, just as there was in taking wooden clubs too far to the left foot, of taking short irons back to the right. The body is inclined to sway back to the right to enable the player to feel he can get behind the ball to lift it, which is the impression some beginners have of the stroke. This is not so. What lifts it is the forward movement of the club with the backspin which the lofted angle of the club provides. The ball should not be played right of centre in normal golf shots. There must always be an encouragement to swing through to the target.

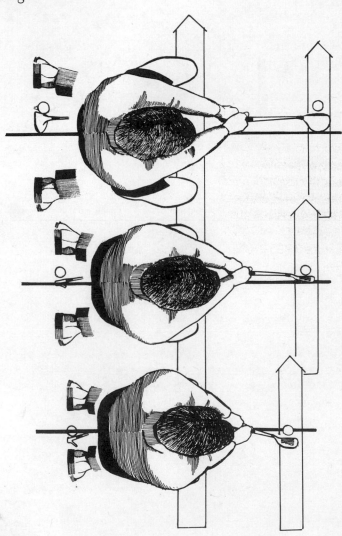

2 ADVANCED

The ball position is used by some good players to help determine the type of shot they require – whether it be that he wishes to move the ball left to right in the air, right to left, hit it high or hit it low, or whether to float it gently downwind or to drive it hard under the wind. The extreme example of such action would be that the ball, if played back behind centre of the feet, would be struck a descending blow which would reduce the effective loft of the club and would result in a low trajectory. The opposite would be to play the ball well forward to a position opposite the left foot from a high tee peg and waft it off upwards from behind, giving it plenty of height.

Whereas in the beginner's simple range of ball positions there are only three alternatives – all woods some two inches inside of the left foot, long irons just ahead of centre of the feet, and the short irons from opposite the centre of the two feet – the more experienced player has a wider basic range to select from.

The driver takes a completely individual placing from which no other shot is played, as far forward as the inside of the left foot, because this is a club designed to catch the ball on the upswing of the follow-through.

The rest of the clubs divide the remaining area which extends only as far back as the centre of the feet. The wedge and 9 iron are back markers, just ahead are the 7 and 8, and midway between the driver and the wedge are the 4, 5 and 6 irons. The pattern of moving forward is created by the enthusiasm for power and the additional length of shaft in the clubs. The long irons and fairway woods share a well-forward position but always inside that private domain of the driver. It might be argued that sharing an area must be wrong, but in the modern set of clubs and in the modern game of golf, many types of long fairway shots are played. Two clubs which have become very popular with good players are a 5 wood and a 1 iron, producing in the former a wood which is nearly an iron and in the latter an iron which is nearly a wood. There is so much variety of stroke available in this range that I have deliberately linked the two together in my drawing.

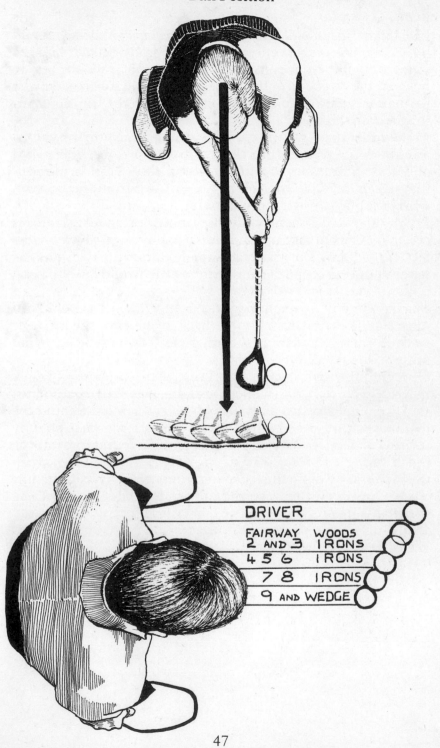

DRIVER

FAIRWAY WOODS
2 AND 3 IRONS

4 5 6 IRONS

7 8 IRONS

9 AND WEDGE

3 BASE OF ARC

One might imagine that the centre of the base of the arc would be at a point opposite the centre of the body, but in fact the swing in motion moves its base forward and takes the centre towards the direction of the target. This is the sole reason why the ball is struck before the club enters the turf in the good-quality iron shot.

Many golfers have gone to great lengths to adjust their swing in an effort to achieve the 'ball the turf' iron shot, when in fact it is only the natural forward movement of the swing in momentum which takes the base of the arc forward from the position where the player originally placed his clubhead.

For the above reasons, no full shot under normal conditions is ever played from a position behind opposite of centre of the feet. A player would simply be unable to move forward as the natural process of good swing requires. He would have to hang back with his weight to strike the ball.

Placing the ball is much more accurate with the experienced player – the driver from the left heel at one end, the pitching wedge from the centre and the other clubs in sequence at what must be about half-inch intervals.

Opposite the left heel is an important statement. Many players, often top tournament players, play the ball for tee shots very far forward and this can be dangerous. Should the foot be slightly turned out, and most people do have slightly turned-out feet, the ball can be accidentally found to be not so much opposite the left foot as opposite the left toe. Only when they are asked to spin the toe in to right angles to the target line do they find out just how far the ball position has crept forward, with damaging results.

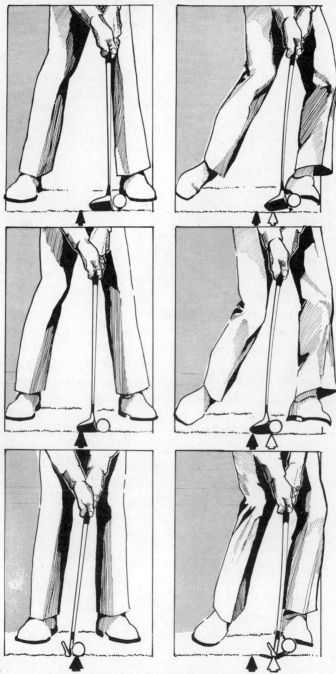

STANCE
The black arrows show the base of a slow arc.
The white arrows show the base of an arc in momentum.

6

Stance

WIDTH OF STANCE

It is essential that a player chooses the correct width of stance because the distance the feet are apart has great influence on the creative ability of the swing.

It is generally accepted that the stance should be wide for the driver and long clubs, and narrow for the short irons. This acceptance is often based on the aggressive attitude to the full shot. Whilst this is correct thinking, there is another very good reason for the alteration of width between the feet.

The right leg could be called the 'igniter of hand action', for it is a barrier to the body turn in the backswing. When this barrier is reached, the turn becomes difficult and the hands and wrists are encouraged more into the stroke.

The driver probably uses the least creative hand work and has the greatest amount of body turn. A broad stance is to be encouraged, for the club has to be well on its way to a complete backswing when the resistance of the right leg is met. There is little need then for individual hand action.

At the other extreme, with the wedge, the right leg is encountered as a barrier very quickly since the stance is narrow. This forces more wrist action to take place, steepening the plane of the upswing, all correct for the club. The sand iron stance is not only narrow but has the right foot and leg forward. This causes an even earlier 'ignition' of hands and wrists, forcing the club into even more steepness and causing the ball to be hit across.

The sand iron is a perfect example of using the stance width adjustment to force early hand and wrist action. Should a player need additional height of flight with a longer club, then a narrower stance should be used. To obtain a low trajectory flight a broader stance will dull the wrists and take out the backspinning punch.

51

2 DIRECTION OF STANCE: SQUARE: OPEN: CLOSED

Taking up one's stance is a very serious business, for a player may make a type of stroke happen by the way he intentionally places his feet or he can be forced into a result which an accidentally inaccurate stance has made inevitable. There are three directions in which a golfer may place his feet and these are known in golfing terms as square, which would be direct at the target, open, to the left of target and closed, to the right of target.

One might feel safe in assuming that top players would all stand square, but this is not the case. Attempting to stand square might accidentally lead to a slight mistake being made in one direction or the other and that is not positive enough for them. They prefer to make a choice of just one direction or the other, then they can feel confident of what has to be done with the ball to propel it to the target. Of the players who adopt this policy, the modern golf swing which prefers a much simpler and less active wrist action, has produced a ratio of about ten to one who are open. The more wristy swing used some years ago, unfortunately still indulged in by too many teachers in Great Britain, preferred the stance a little closed and the ball was hit by a rolling clubface. By standing a fraction left a player can see exactly where the ball has to be hit and his wrists may remain more solid through the strike, driving on towards the target.

To stand perfectly square would suit any method of swinging, but a golfer only has to line up his feet to a target and lay a club on the grass along the line of his toes to find out just how difficult square is to find. I personally prefer my pupils to be just a degree open. It is beneficial to the swing, giving a stronger right leg to support the backswing and leaving a clear way for the follow through. Standing closed allows overswinging going back, and turns the left leg into a barrier for the through swing.

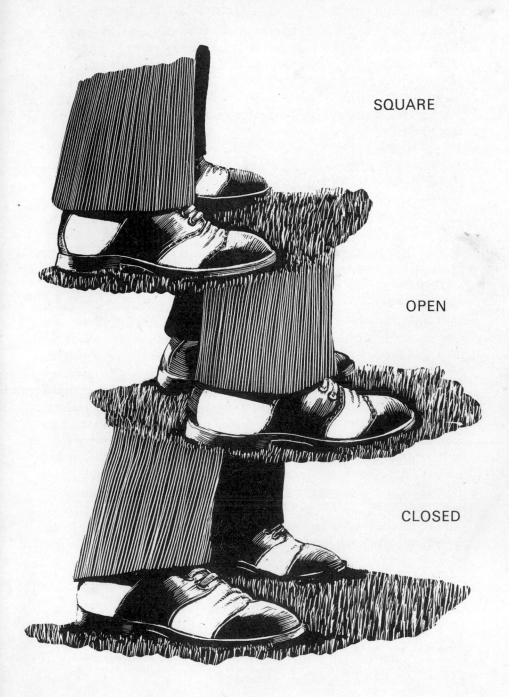

SQUARE

OPEN

CLOSED

3 OPEN STANCE

On a trip to Laurel Valley as a member of the British party of officials, affectionately known as the 'hangers on', I made a careful study of the American Ryder Cup Team, particularly their placing of the feet for direction. Almost to a man they stood open, left of target. The top American players are more uniform in their method of swinging and open suits the less wristy action through the ball.

The player I have illustrated from that team is Lee Trevino, who must be the open-stanced player of all time. He does not stand a few degrees left, he stands miles to the left. This is so that he may drive the ball all the farther from him, maintaining the face of the club to the target all the longer. He is a fantastic golfer who demonstrates the advantage that open stance has over closed, for being forced to go after the ball must be better than going round one. However, his extreme must not be copied, for he has exaggerated a stance which suits him and not many others. Standing too open forces the backswing to turn very flat in its plane and encourages a great deal of body movement, which is only suited to a shorter physique and requires great leg work to keep it under control. He has it all, but not many do.

Strangely enough, Scotland's Norman Wood beat Lee in the singles, having spent a season getting rid of an open stance which used to make him push the ball. But then Norman is probably six inches taller and standing too open at his height had been flattening his swing plane.

I made a similar study of the American team in the following Ryder Cup matches played at Lytham St. Annes and found, with the exception of one player, the rest of the team had their feet to the left of the target. I, fortunately, had the job of refereeing the first singles match that Nick Faldo has played representing his country, against the American Tom Watson, at that time holder of the British Open title, and was pleased to note the care both players attached to having a stance which was slightly left of the target. Both of them adopting the procedure of standing behind the ball, directly in line with the ball and the target and then walking around slowly so that there was no danger of crossing the target line with their toes and having a closed stance.

4 CLOSED STANCE

The greatest exponent of all time of the closed stance was Bobby Locke of South Africa. When teaching, I have to keep tongue in cheek when I tell beginners that nobody can play well with their feet to the right of the target. He was one of the greatest ever controllers of the ball's flight and used a method which nobody would dare build into a pupil, and it may seem a bit strange using the action of a world-class player to describe why a closed stance should not be used.

With the feet aiming off to the right, the path of the swing will be very much from in to out of a straight line to the target. Common sense would see that a ball hit from this movement would travel to the right but unfortunately it is not common sense that takes over, it is reflex! Reflex tells the clubhead that the target is around the corner to the left of where the club is swinging and the hands turn the wrists over so that the clubhead may give the ball new instructions.

The closed stance usually creeps up on a person who believes he is standing square. Gently at first he aims off and the reflexes turn the ball in the air so in fact it flies left of target. The next stage of the disease is that the player aims his stance a little further to the right and the clubhead has to roll even more until eventually it begins to prepare for the rolling through the ball by rolling away on the backswing. The hands are now doing a 'repair job' to hit the ball.

With all due respect to Bobby Locke, whom I had the privilege of meeting at his home club Observatory in Johannesburg, who could get backspin on a hooking flight, this is no way to place the feet. A closed stance is a must not.

5 Open Preferred to Closed

At the top of a backswing, an angle is created between the line of the club's shaft and the line of the left arm. This angle may be very acute and it is the angle of leverage. Whilst the line of the shaft remains behind the line of the arm, leverage still exists. The moment the line of the shaft passes the line of the arm, the power will be spent and the clubhead speed will drop. All incentive for the club will be over.

This is the true reason why the closed stance is discouraged and the open stance is preferred. The illustration of the closed foot position demonstrates the journey the hands are required to make to get the clubface to hit the ball towards the target. The widest point of the downward path of the hands will come well before the ball, and once the widest point in the downswing has been passed the clubhead must then be in advance of the hands, and the all-important lead of the left arm over the club shaft is lost. This is commonly known as hitting early.

The open stance, on the other hand, encourages the left arm to keep going in order that the ball may be hit away from the off-set line of the feet. This means that the clubhead is still chasing the left arm as it passes through the ball. The leverage is contained throughout the whole downswing and the widest point of the down arc is yet to come.

A player must not fold before he hits the ball and that is what closed insists he does. The downswing of the slightly open stance may give the impression that the ball shall be pushed away to the right of the target but one has to bear in mind that the centrifugal throw of the clubhead works for the open stance, squaring the clubface as it rushes to catch up with the line of the left arm. In the case of the closed stance, this throw becomes an additional disaster putting more stress on the collapsed left wrist.

If a golfer could stand absolutely square on to the target every time, then that would be the perfect line-up, but if he cannot be absolutely sure, the slightly open is best.

6 RELATION OF FEET TO SHOULDERS

The path on which the swing flows is dictated by the line of the shoulders. Great care then must be taken so that the shoulders point in a direct line to the target. The alteration of the ball position for the various lengths of club is a main cause of disturbance to the shoulder line.

If a ball is being played forward as in the case of a driver, the left shoulder is tempted to turn away to the left of the target, bringing the right shoulder forward. The swing path in this case would be led across the ball, causing a side spin to be imparted on the ball, slicing it away to the right.

With a ball being placed back, either for a short iron or perhaps a shot being brought back to be hit under the wind, the right shoulder is forced to pull back, bringing the left forward and so aiming them off to the right. The path of the swing would be made too much in to out, encouraging an early hand action, and creating a right-to-left spin which would rotate the ball to the left in a hooking flight. Alteration of ball position must therefore be coupled with close attention being paid to the line of the shoulders, to see that they are aimed at the target.

The same attention must be paid by a player who chooses either to open or close his line of stance. I have illustrated Johnny Miller, the American Ryder Cup player, who is another renowned for standing with his feet open to the target and who is also noted for the care he takes to be certain that, although the feet are several degrees to the left, the shoulders are square on.

To Alex
Best wishes and
This is great stuff

John Miller

ALEX HAY

61

7 INTRODUCTION TO SIDEHILL LIES

Most practice areas, practice grounds and driving ranges are on level ground. Obviously there is not much point in trying to hit a ball from a hill until it can be hit successfully from the flat. So it is that many beginners find all the work they have been doing on building a swing disrupted by the fact that golf courses are often hilly places where their feet and the ball never seem to find the same level.

The greatest difficulty of the hill is that gravity says lean into the slope when the golf swing requires that we in fact lean out from it. To try and maintain the same body position regardless of the level of the ball would need a set of clubs where the length of the shaft and the angle the head is fitted to it would be adjustable.

It is essential that the base of the clubhead is permitted to be flat to the slope and the body leaned to suit it. The secret of playing on hills is simply to argue with gravity but never argue with the hill. Allow the hill to rule the swing plane and its length of arc, and to determine the direction of the flight of the ball.

There are occasions when a slope is so steep that heed has to be paid to gravity or we would have players toppling head over heels into ponds and bunkers. When such a slope is encountered, a full shot will not be possible and only a small lofted stroke would be used. The next few pages apply to the more reasonable hillsides.

8 STANDING ABOVE THE BALL

The player must attempt to get his balance point leaning as near to right angles to the slope as possible. This would mean that his body should tilt forward when common sense would suggest he should lean backwards to counteract the slope. By leaning forward the base of the club may rest on the turf and the hands will find a position where they can hit the ball. This would be eliminated if the player leaned backwards to counteract the hill.

There is a price to pay when the body leans forward and that is that the forward muscles of the legs and the strength of the toes are used as props of strength. I have illustrated by the black stripes just where the pressure would be felt and this pressure must be maintained throughout the swing. Being supports, the legs are limited in their movement and so a limited turn of the body is allowed, casting the swing into an upright plane, and reducing the length of the arc – a combination which limits the development of power and makes the ball likely to be hit slightly across. In addition, there must be a lack of momentum of swing towards the target so the base of the swing will remain very central, and for this reason the ball is played opposite the middle of the feet.

Because of the restrictions of movement, a player should allow more club than he feels necessary for the distance to be covered but should always bear in mind that sometimes from a steep hill it pays to position the ball rather than attack a difficult target.

The ball will fly to the right from this situation mainly because the resting of the sole of the club on the turf so angles the loft of the clubface that it can only spin the ball upwards in a direction which is at right angles to the slope of the ground. In the drawing, the black line shows the direction the sloping clubhead will despatch the ball as opposed to the dotted line which would apply on level ground.

9 STANDING BELOW THE BALL

The player must attempt to get his balance point to lean towards right angles to the slope. The body weight would in this stroke be set back, using the back muscles of the legs and the heels to sit on, and there it must be maintained. His hands and wrists will rise and the sole-plate of the club will find itself level with the sloping ground. For a player to lean forward to balance himself with gravity, his hands and wrists would have to lower towards his knees.

The black stripes in the drawing show where the pressure is taken up and, as in all sidehill strokes, the original pressure of adjusted balance must be held throughout the action. From this leaning-back position the swing plane will be flattened, and with the spine becoming more upright, a greater freedom of shoulder turn is made available. This should be encouraged. The swing, on its flatter plane, will take on a sweeping effect and so care should be taken that the ball is positioned in a forward position.

A full shoulder turn and a flat plane are factors which contribute to pulling the ball to the left and these added to the angle I have drawn in a heavy black line, as opposed to the dotted right angle, would mean that the ball must spin in an 'off to the left' direction. The player must not argue! He must aim to the right and allow for the leftward movement of the ball.

Strangely enough, this type of slope encourages the fullness of swing that other slopes do not, so that even with the legs acting as props, and provided a player aims right, he can be quite adventurous with his choice of clubs seeking long distances.

10 DOWNHILL LIE

Playing down a slope always gives the player the feeling he should hang back with his weight to help get the ball up. Disastrous thinking, because this is the stroke where ground is most likely to be contacted before the ball. This is the main factor to be removed. The body must lean into the downhill leg so that the club may swing upwards into its backswing and safely downwards to the ball. The stripes in the drawing show where the pressure is and where it must remain throughout the stroke.

Leaning into the downhill support, which is the left leg, and maintaining right angles to turf rather than to gravity, enables a tremendous amount of shoulder turn and fullness of backswing which can be dangerous, with a player feeling he has brought his arc up sharply. However, there is safety in the fact that a club with extra loft will be used.

The angle of the clubhead travelling down the hill as shown with the black line as opposed to the dotted line will send the ball off in a lower trajectory. A ball will travel farther on its lower flight and a more lofted club gives the player confidence and safety.

The player must not argue with his fuller backswing and restricted follow-through movement but must position the ball back and let the extra loft lift the ball.

11 UPHILL LIE

The argument with gravity is very important with an uphill stroke. The natural movement of the body during the swing would be to move forward into the slope as if to help the ball to climb. This must be resisted. The back leg is deliberately bent to allow the body line to be right-angled to the turf, and that bent leg has to hold as the prop throughout the swing. I have illustrated with the stripes just in which area the pressure is maintained.

With the right leg holding the weight back on its own, a full turn of the body is restricted and the backswing will be shortened. However, greater freedom of follow through will be enjoyed but this enjoyment comes with the clubface swinging up the hill as I have shown with the black line and as can be seen, the clubface has acquired more degrees of loft than the one on the dotted line of right angle. The ball is going to climb with a higher trajectory.

The player must not argue but must use a longer club, calculating for the loss of distance the upflight will create. With the backswing being short, as a result of the supporting right leg acting as a resistance but with the ensuing freedom of the up-and-through surge to the finish, the ball is played in a forward position. Occasionally, and particularly if the slope is very severe, the body weight is held back on the bent right leg and one may have difficulty in any forward movement, the ball then being likely to fly to the left as well as gain height.

7

Posture

1 INTRODUCTION

The beauty of golf is that it may be played by people of all ages and people of all shapes and sizes. Because of the game's handicapping system, players of lesser ability may compete with their betters which is not possible in any other ball game that I know of. Unfortunately, this gives the impression to non-golfers that playing the game is no more strenuous than walking, and that the golf swing is not an athletic feat. Anyone under this impression would receive the shock of his sweet life if he stood on a practice ground within a few feet of Jack Nicklaus, Arnold Palmer, or Gary Player. Every muscle is used to generate a power that does not seem humanly possible and the ball is propelled further and faster than in any other sport.

The golf swing is an athletic movement which is fortunately tied up with rhythm and feel rather than just physical strength and it requires co-ordination and balance, only found from correct posture. If golfers paid more heed to posture as they lined up to a ball they would be on the way to creating a better swing, and would gain extra distance that proper balance would bring about.

One of the things I have never understood was the statement "get the weight back on the heels" as though this was a standard position for every stroke. It certainly is not, and as far as I know in most other athletic activity placing the weight on the heels kills movement.

A very short man with a long shafted club would be the only person, owing to the flat arc which his swing would require, who would possibly sit back on his heels. Gary Player is someone whose address often gives this impression, but he is small and his search for a wider arc flattens him even more. Most

72

other tournament players in fact give the impression that there is a definite tilt towards the balls of the feet, from where, strangely enough, most athletic movement stems. They are careful to flex the legs so that a lean is not created.

The Mechanics of Golf

In the game of golf the posture is a very important factor. Posture means the placing of the trunk of the body and the limbs into a position which allows and encourages them to function fluidly, maintaining the best point of balance, whilst bearing in mind that they are to be guided by the needs of an arc angled according to the club in use.

The blessing of it all is that the arms and hands are easily guided when the club base is placed on the turf and that the difference of lengths in the clubs is the measuring stick which tells the player just how his posture would be in best use for each stroke. There is a pattern for correct posture. The information is passed from the shaft angle through the arms to the trunk, then down through the legs to the feet. The complete procedure to arrive at 'good posture' would be as follows:

> Rest the sole of the club evenly on the turf.
> Allow the shoulders to lean forward, the trunk bending from the waist.
> Flex the knee and ankle joints only enough to give suppleness of movement, taking up the balance evenly in the feet.

Do not reverse the process by:

> Sitting down on the heels, leaning the body weight backwards and then, with the spine all erect, attempt to arch the wrists in order to get the clubhead to the ball.

To take up one's body and leg positions before introducing the clubhead to ball and turf sounds an almost unbelievable procedure but unfortunately it is a very common practice.

At the beginning, before correct routine has been established, achieving good posture may cause a feeling of tension but this is easily relieved by simply straightening up, taking a breath to relax, then by gently leaning back into correct posture, the pressure all gone. Jack Nicklaus is no beginner and he likes to have a last-minute straighten and a deep breath before settling to hit the ball.

A close study of the top players shows the average posture to be knees above the shoe laces, with the shoulders in a direct line above the toes. This position will vary slightly with the shoulders coming further forward for the shorter irons and then backing up for the driver, but it is nonetheless a good guide to good posture for an athletic golf swing. To me, Bobby Cole of South Africa is the perfect example of good posture.

2 THE TRUNK

When a player places the sole of the longest club, his driver, on the turf the arms need very little lowering to reach the long shaft and tell the trunk to relax and stay reasonably upright.

If the player placed the sole of his shortest club, his wedge, on the turf it is so short-shafted, and so angled that his hands and arms have to be lowered, bringing the trunk over on quite a slant.

The circle made by the club is around the top of the trunk, and it is tilted only by the angle of lean the length of the shaft has demanded. Imagine the shoulders as the spokes of a wheel and the spine as the axle. Then the angle on which the shoulders would spin would be determined entirely by the slant of the spine.

If a player is to have the correct shallow angle of tilt for his long-shafted driver then the spine must be allowed to be made more erect by it. It is simply the leaning forward of that spine to reach the shorter handle of the wedge which tilts the swing arc more upright.

The correct spinal angle at the setting-up to the ball is the only factor which says whether the left shoulder should come around in front of the chin when the backswing is made or whether it should come well under the chin.

One of golf's greatest tragedies of misinterpretation is that the left shoulder should go down to make a backswing. I have seen players making a swing, or what they call a swing, by lowering the left shoulder for the backswing and then the right for the follow through. These positions must be relative to the angle of the trunk at the address. The arc made by a baseball player is clearly seen to be almost perfectly horizontal. This is only because his spine is vertical. What a pity the youth of England play cricket instead of baseball. Bending over a cricket bat which is vertical to the ground makes natural movement almost impossible, whereas the horizontal arc of the baseball bat is nature encouraged. There must be no conscious lowering of either shoulder, their angled arc being taken care of in the correct posture of the trunk.

3 Legs and Feet

The legs and feet are used to give balance to the spinning-top half of the body, to take the transfer of load from out in front at the address to around the back for the backswing, then out to the front again to hit the ball, and still be ready to support all the aggression of the follow through. At the same time they have to give forth a bit of power, though not as much as is written about. It is essential that they are properly flexed without creating an argument for the position of the trunk.

With the spine pushed more erect by the longer shaft it would be quite in order for the legs to flex at the knees, almost giving the impression that the player is slightly sitting, and with a small man the weight might even be set back towards the heels.

When the spine is leaning forward to the shorter club the knees would be less bent and the body weight would be more to the toes than the heels.

Some time ago the statement was made that a player should feel that he was sitting on a seatstick. It should also have been stated that although it could apply to a very short man through most of his clubs, it would apply in the case of a tall man only with his longest clubs. Correct posture is most important and height has great bearing on posture. The only standardizing is that the club in use must determine the angle of the spine. The spine must determine the angle of the swing's arc. The amount of flex in the legs ties in accordingly.

A tall man sitting on his seatstick using a shorter club would have his spine so erect that he would never find his correct angle of arc. He would be forced to swing flat. This is the prime cause of shanking. Swinging a club back at an angle flatter than correct posture would mean that the clubface would be rolled open, and the return journey would require the re-roll which throws the face of the club outwards, causing the dreaded socket of the club to strike the ball.

An ideal average point in the feet to carry the weight would be between the heel and the ball of each foot.

Posture

4 THE HEAD

A chapter on posture could hardly be complete without a mention of the head. Whilst it contains one or two very impo: tant items such as the brain and the eyes, it is asked to do very little in the actual swing other than to keep still and mind its own business. However, it can do immense damage to the swing if it is incorrectly positioned at the address and this is why it must be brought up under the heading of posture.

The amount the head should lean forward would be determined by the forward tilt of the spine. Not much for the driver, and the eyes would be looking out to the ball. Quite a lot for the wedge, with the eyes cast downward.

The turning of the head at the address can help or hinder a backswing, for should a player look at the ball from the right corner of his right eye he would encourage a lateral movement to his right before his swing momentum could have any effect on turning the trunk. This movement is one of the main causes of swaying.

Looking at the ball from the left corner of the left eye has the effect of taking the swing straight into turn and is often used very successfully by less supple people who find the turning of the trunk a bit difficult. Coupled with more footwork, it is to be encouraged for older golfers.

A head must never under any circumstances be leaned either to the right or to the left. This would create a deforming of the top of the spine and would completely damage any chance of good swinging.

In the initial search for good posture the head should be encouraged to 'feel tall' at the address, where it will give an awareness of maintaining good position. Should the chin slouch into the chest, a lateral movement will certainly be encouraged.

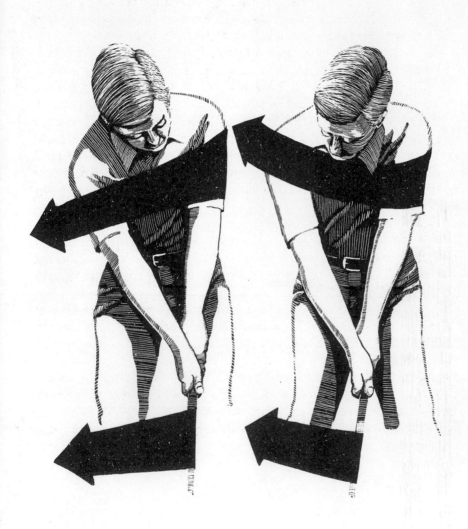

8
Set-up

Throughout golf, different people are associated with various parts of the swing – for example, Ben Hogan, when he explained 'plane of swing' more clearly than had ever been done before. In my mind 'set-up' has two great players associated with it and there is a similarity about the two. One is Peter Thomson and the other Gary Player. The similarity is that both swing the club in a very shallow, flat plane. It may seem obvious that Player should swing this way since he is a short man, but why should Thomson who is quite average in height? The fact is that he has very short arms and made up for this by having his clubs made one inch longer. The combination of these two factors caused him to have his wrists higher at the address which give him the swing plane of a smaller man.

The last thing I wish to convey is that to have good set-up one must have a flat swing. A swing angle is determined by the height and physique of the player. What these two did was to widen the arc of the swing, Player to its limit, refusing to believe that a small man should hit the ball shorter distances. With the widening, great risk of an inconsistent return to the ball was encountered, and the way this was overcome was by placing great stress on informing the muscles of just how they should feel and how they should react when they passed through the strike. When lining up to the ball, they place themselves as near to the position in which they would wish to be when actually hitting the ball. They set themselves into a mould which is easily found on the return journey and that is exactly why the expression set-up took over from 'addressing' the ball.

The old attitude of addressing the ball was to line the club up to the ball and then swish it back and forth above the ball, as though swatting flies, as a means of limbering up mind and body to greater rhythm. Thomson and Player made it more than that. It is now the point from where a player may build into mind and muscle the type of swing he wishes to make, it is the build-up of support and consistency, and it makes so clear just how the player should feel back through the ball. Watching Gary Player is the ultimate experience of seeing the eventual path of a swing pre-determined in the set-up.

The Mechanics of Golf

1 PETER THOMSON

My first encounter with the expression set-up was in an aeroplane, a propellered one, returning from the Irish Hospitals Tournament. Peter Thomson's companion had left his seat and I did not waste a moment filling it. Although he was not much older than I his skill, experience, knowledge and willingness to explain had me spellbound. His colleague, on his return, was directed to another seat so that we could talk. I questioned and he answered for the entire flight.

Our conversation was almost exactly the one he had with Henry Longhurst some years later when, in *The Times*, Henry did more for set-up by re-telling it to his readers. The left side of the body, the left hand, and the left arm dominate the set-up. The left hand places the clubhead behind the ball so that from a frontal view there exists an almost straight line from left shoulder down through the arm and the shaft of the club to the ball. (I stress the frontal view because if my memory serves me right, *The Times* did not, and many people made a straight line of shoulder to clubhead on a view from the direction of the target. This made the wrist rigid and was not the intention. It may have been overlooked since Thomson had short arms and used longer clubs and his line would look straighter than most from the target view. Nevertheless, this would be a dangerous straightness for an average player). Whatever the right hand and arm had to do to get onto the handle had absolutely no influence on the firm left side. The left-side domination is the mould from which good plane and wide arc stem.

The reason more good did not come from the Henry Longhurst article was because the dominating left-side set-up was clearly designed for a swing where the wrist action would be working 'square' in the 'plane' of the swing (detailed in their own chapters of this book) and the British were not ready for this at the time. The wristier, more open-faced golf swing did not like the stabilizing effect of this set-up which seemed to stifle the wrist joints. This was a great pity because wrist action is very necessary in a golf swing. Peter Thomson's method was ready to make better wrist action and, thank God, it is beginning to get through at last. What better way to influence the hand action than the mental and physical preparation which good set-up provides and encourages.

84

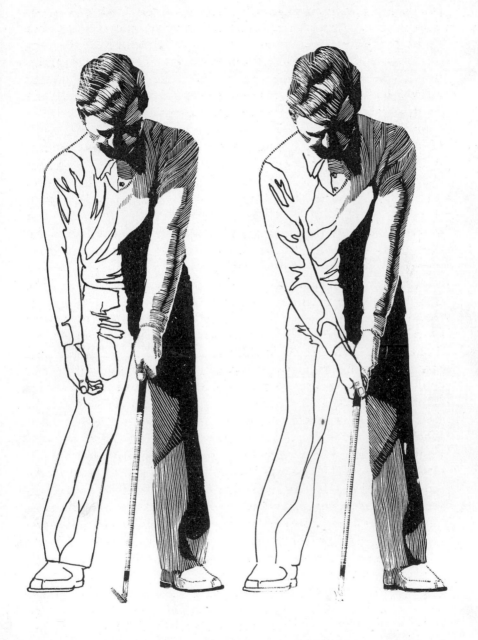

2. GARY PLAYER AND THE K SHAPE

Quite recently I had the pleasure of a very long talk on the subject of the golf swing with Gary Player which started at the Breakfast table and went on long into the afternoon and much of the discussion was taken up with the importance which Gary attaches to his set-up position. He stretches his swing over as wide an arc as anyone in the game. He is often criticized for 'falling off' the follow through but this is not bad swinging, it is simply the result of an aggression and great courage putting in an effort that the good swing cannot cope with. Fortunately the ball is well on its way to the target when his position yields to the pressure. He is the perfect example of a player who needs a good set-up. He really has to have the muscular memory of the point he must pass through to hit the ball.

His position at set-up is virtually the one golf teachers call the letter K. It is a K in reverse and like Peter Thomson shows the concern that the left side dominates. Also like Thomson the domination carries him wide, shallow, and strong into a backswing with the wrists in a perfect square position.

Player's contribution went beyond that of Thomson. It was to take set-up from just left side and left arm, which was sufficient for the calmer, more balanced swing of the Australian, into the legs. His endeavour to get 'still more' out of himself made the consistency of retaining his arc much more vulnerable. He showed that by creating a forward press of his right leg in towards the left, he not only gave the backswing the initiative to start but showed the legs just how they were to feel when the club was striking the ball. So it is then that he is the prime example given by teachers when the set-up is the subject. He prepares for everything and we should not be fooled into thinking that his shoulder roll at the finish is anything other than aggression. It is certainly not bad swing, for he is too well set-up for that. Anyway, one of the characteristics of the left-side-dominated set-up is that the left shoulder is built up and withstands the right arm and shoulder which show up in weaker set-ups, the cause of many bad swings.

Set-up

3 THE Y SHAPE

Another letter of the alphabet which comes into set-up is the letter Y. It is used to describe approximately the line of the arms to the shaft when a more flexible or wristy type of swing is required.

In the case of a lady golfer or a man with weaker hands, wrists or legs, or for someone who has difficulty in turning the trunk, the dominating left-side set-up described as a letter K would be quite out of the question. Golf may be played well by most individuals provided the technique used is suited both physically and mentally. So, weaker persons creating a Y shape should realize that, whilst a left-side-dominated set-up is not for them, their necessary Y shape has its limitations and is vulnerable.

If a line were drawn down the left arm at the line-up to the ball, it would continue to a spot behind the clubhead. The wrist is therefore buckling in order to place the clubhead to the ball. This means that the club will have to swing past the authority of the left arm on the downswing before it can strike the ball,

and this is the prime cause of fluffed shots. Players who have to use the Y shape should add another knuckle to the prescribed two of the left-hand grip. Three knuckles showing will help support the wrist and get the clubhead more quickly to the ball. On occasions the Y shape is used by a strong player wishing to use extra wrist action for a short, lofted stroke such as a bunker shot. In this case the softened wrist action is correct. Unfortunately it is quite common to see a good player who dominates his wooden club play with a well-supported left side accidentally place himself in a Y shape when the ball position of an iron stroke goes more central. His left arm comes back with the ball. This is incorrect. Whilst there must be a slight come-back of the arm, the left arm should stay forward of the blade. If care is not taken a strong player will find he is slapping at his iron strokes. Unlike the weaker person, who adjusts the grip to suit the weakness, the stronger player has a grip geared to a simpler process through the ball.

4 INCORRECT SET-UP

Like most parts of a golf swing, too much thought can have the effect of making the movements artificial. A left-side-dominated set-up is no exception. Even the term SET-UP has a ring of tension about it and it would be sad if anyone allowed what could be a very beneficial conditioner for good swing to become a monster which locks the swing in the grip of rigidity.

I would be the last to deny that the left-sided set-up is not natural. I have watched enough beginners holding the club in their right hand and teeing up the ball with their left, then placing the clubhead to the ball with the right hand, the arm reaching out the distance, only to leave the left hand and arm to fit on as best they can. This is the natural way for a right-handed person to prepare to hit an object. But I have also watched the world's great players to see the opposite take place: the left hand on the handle whilst the right tees up the ball, the left hand and arm gauging the reach, then the right hand and arm being added. This does not mean that these fellows are not natural golfers but that they have learned that on many occasions method plays a great part in consistent performance.

The width of a hand means that the right hand has some four inches further to reach than the left. If a player assesses his reach to the ball by his right hand and arm, then his left would have to buckle in order to lose four inches. If it did not buckle then it would have to force the left shoulder to turn out of line to the left, and so damage the path of the swing.

Should the distance of reach be assessed by left hand and arm, the only way of getting the right hand down the extra four inches is by lowering the right side, by flexing the right leg, and by lowering the right shoulder. These are exactly the positions described by a K-shaped set-up, and the only way to be sure the shoulder line stays on target.

My illustration shows, by means of a beam of light from the direction of the target, how a player would look if he started his set-up by his right side, the trunk turning open, as opposed to a player who has gone through the correct procedure of setting up.

9

Backswing

1 THE PLANE OF SWING

Up to this point, I feel that not too many golf teachers would argue with the order in the sequence of parts of the swing I have introduced, but from this point onwards there may be some who would. The foundation has been laid with set-up being the launching pad for the swing, and the argument amongst teachers is, just what starts it all off? Some would, at this stage, commence with a programme of hand and wrist exercises, insisting that it is a game of hands and wrists hitting the ball, using the swinging arc as the platform. In my opinion this cannot be done without knowing where the platform is. The platform is the most important part, particularly with a beginner. After all, the swinging weight of a club with its subsequent leverage will almost certainly, provided a correct grip has been taught, create enough angle between arms and shaft by way of the wrist joints, to create its own acceleration.

It is not my intention to knock the very important training of correct hand action but simply to get priority right. The search for creative hands and wrists is quite a risky business for a beginner. What they are looking for as they hinge their wrist joints immediately on leaving the ball is leverage, and this is formed very quickly by a rolling of the wrist joints, causing the face of the club to rotate open too quickly. The wrists then re-rotate to create an impact, calculating that they will have the clubface squared at impact before it closes over as the rotation continues its process.

The beginner is liable to acquire a feeling of individualism of hands and wrists which is not conducive to co-ordinated movement. Normally anyone learning this method would be using a very lofted club which gives a false illusion of success, the additional angle of clubface loft making allowance for the narrowness of the arc.

The correct method of finding hand action is only to search for it within the protection of the plane of the swing – the platform! When a swing plane has been located by a beginner – bearing in mind that whilst the search is on, actual leverage and good grip will be encouraging healthy hand and wrist action of its own – then a platform for consistency will have been built.

2 WHAT IS PLANE?

The clear understanding of swing plane took tremendous strides when Ben Hogan and the artist Anthony Ravielli explained how a plate-glass window, if laid from the ball onto a golfer's shoulders, by means of his head popping through a hole in the centre of the pane, gave the angle at which the left arm should swing. By brushing the underside of the glass during the backswing it would arrive at the top in direct line of leverage to the ball which exactly describes plane. It is the direct line of leverage from which there is no short cut down.

I use the expression short cut because if one imagines the arms or the hands breaking up through that pane of glass then the short cut available would be a steep descent onto, or even across the ball. If the arms or the wrists flattened below the level of the pane, the swing would be forced narrow and too tight to the body, creating another short cut.

There is a line of leverage, shallower on longer clubs than shorter ones because it is relative to the spinal tilt. At the top of a backswing, if the body is correctly wound it will have built up muscles for the downswing. If muscles did not have to be built up we could all start from the top, with no need for a risky backswing and all the necessary timing that goes with it. Yes, muscular leverage is there, and at this point the muscular pressure is felt under the arm socket on the left side, for it is about to pull. On the right side it is the top of the shoulder which has been developed, for the muscles of the right side are built to push. Therefore if a line is drawn from top of right shoulder through bottom of left it should find the ball. And if that line were continued up the other way it would find the shaft.

The subject of my drawing is Hale Irwin, who is a model exponent of being in plane at the top of the backswing with everything in direct line with no short cut available. His journey back to the ball is as near a perfect reproduction of the upswing as made by anyone in golf.

The true description of plane is *the swinging of the arc to a point at the top of the backswing where a direct line of leverage requires only a straightforward reversal of that arc to find the ball*.

ALEXHAY.

3 IN SEARCH OF PLANE

As soon as an understanding of the sequence so far is reached, that is grip, blade, ball position, stance, posture and set-up, a novice should immediately commence the search for correct plane to establish quickly a mental picture of a swing path to take him into line of direct leverage for a good return to and through the ball.

To find a mental picture of many parts in motion is an impossibility. Stretching the mind only over the minimum of parts is the only way to keep the picture clear.

To find plane a medium iron such as a 6 or 7 is used and three physical areas need concentrating on:

> The left side and shoulder. Already prepared by good set-up.
> The left arm, both hands and the club. Already prepared by correct grip.
> The right hip, to gather up the strain. Already positioned by a good posture.

The player should imagine plane as a channel rather than a line. By turning his left side to the front, the only tilt being created by the spinal tilt, he should swing his arms, hands and the club off in search of the channel.

There is no need to worry about hand action because the initial search to establish plane only requires a part swing and any early hand action is provided by natural movement created by the swinging weight of the club on wrist joints hingeing them in the protection of the channel.

First efforts should be stopped on completion of the initial movement, then the player may turn his head and examine the angle on which the shaft is lying. This should be approximately the angle at which the club stood at set-up although of course it is now upside down.

When a beginner feels that he is beginning to create his angle of plane he should, by a simple means of reversal, transfer the arc to a similar point on his left side. In a very short space of time fluency will creep in and a swinging movement will be forming, the left hip gathering the through swing, just as the right had done on the backswing. Not only is a safe platform being built but traces of healthy footwork will begin to show.

4 INCORRECT SEARCH FOR PLANE

As in every other sport the golf swing evolved and no doubt will continue to, although I cannot see it improving on some of the best swingers we have today. I realize that this is a statement which has been made over each generation, but photographs of yesteryear show elbows and wrists with no regard for plane and the protection it affords. Gradually the wristiness was strengthened as a 'straight left arm' came to the fore and now that wrist action is being contained more square to the plane even more reliability is being found.

Loss of plane is more likely to be found upwards than downwards because the swing at this point is subjected to great pressure and the easiest way to release the pressure would be upwards out of the arc – hence the flying right elbow. A very good example would be to imagine a golfer swinging his arc on the curve of a hat box, the pressure of his left arm containing the pressure of the lid on the slant, in other words the plane. Inside the box is a jack-in-the-box, the pressure pushing up on the lid. If a player should relax then that jack-in-the-box will push itself out and throw his arc up, out and over and the inevitable slice will occur. It is the control of the left arm which will keep the jack-in-the-box well contained until the club gets back towards the ball where that source of power could be released happily through the ball instead of evilly through the top of the backswing.

The first move to find plane was the previously mentioned piece of teaching knowledge Ben Sayers equipped me with when he launched me on my teaching career. "All you have to do to teach the English is put a handkerchief under the right armpit, they are a' too upright anyway". He was of course working on the principle that if a right arm stays tight to the right side of the body the swing cannot lift. At the time this gem was worked out it was accepted that a swing lifting (upwards out of plane) made available the short cut which produced the slice. The harmful effect this stupid idea had was to take away from the swing the domination of the left side which gives the arc its width. The gimmick was the greatest narrower of the swing ever invented and even if it cured the 'high lift' and its resultant slice it produced the flat Scottish swing and its resultant diving hook.

There is no position that a club swung up with the left arm and hand only that is not perfectly acceptable to the placing on of the right hand. This certainly is not the case in reverse. A club swung back tight with the right hand is virtually unreachable with the left, and when it is swung back wide by the right it is unreachable!

A correct plane and all things good in a backswing come from domination of the left side, the left arm, and the left hand.

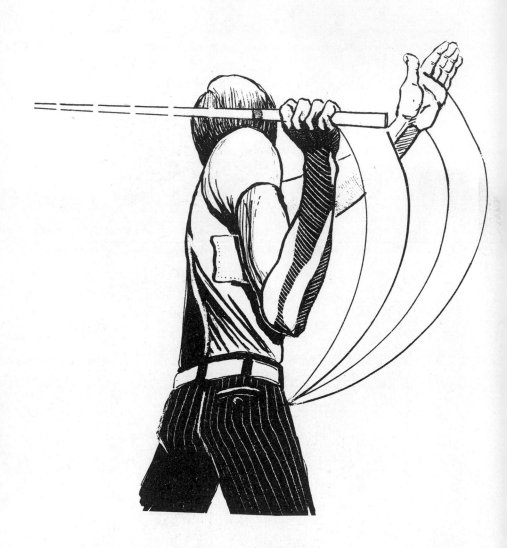

5 HAND AND WRIST ACTION

The work of the hands and wrists in the golf swing is that the hands hinge the wrist joints so as to create an angle between the left arm and the shaft of the club and then to time the undoing of that angle to give the greatest acceleration to the clubhead through the base of the arc.

It is not the job of the hands and wrists to turn the clubhead straight to hit the ball. That is the responsibility of good grip and correct club alignment.

Neither is it the job of the hands and wrists to probe for the ball to be sure the clubface and the ball are on the same level. That is the responsibility of good posture, and correct ball position.

That makes it all sound too simple, as though there is no room or need for skill. Surely, one might claim, if a player had to hit a ball from a very uneven lie, or when he was forced to overreach or crowd close to a ball the player most likely to succeed would be the more talented player, the one with the flair for individual hand action. But it should be borne in mind that these unusual circumstances in fact alter the plane of the swing and it takes an expert to handle the individualism of hand and wrist action out of plane. This is the reason that novices must establish plane first.

The greatest argument in the golf swing is just how the wrists should be hinged by the hands to create the leverage which provides most value through the ball. The top tournament players of the USA make it perfectly clear that provided an angle of 90 degrees between the line of the left arm and the shaft at the top of the backswing is reached this is sufficient. This being the case there is no need for excessive wrist movement which requires more readjusting to get back to the original position it was in at set-up. They have altered the body movement through the strike and on to the finish of the swing to suit their more solid wrist action. This has produced a more balanced share-out of the work load of the golf swing and through better balance the solidity of the strike has made up for any loss that a more supple, more risky use of the wrists may have provided.

Unfortunately, we in Britain were slow to see the swing evolving. There was too great a resemblance between the position of the clubface at the top of the backswing and the position arrived at when the right hand has taken up a 'strong grip' as described in the chapter on grip, where the clubface becomes closed. Unfortunately, 'people in high places' still insist that a more individual use of the wrists by the hands must prevail and the matching body movement should stay. When some of the younger men in the 1950s changed over they were criticized and the criticism was all out of a blindness to accept change. The days of the flowing English swing were over, the shaft well beyond horizontal at the top of the backswing, the hitting up against a firm left side were gone, all unnecessary. The days when the experts, gifted with natural flair, played well and the others sliced their way around were going. All because of one word, square!

When I stated there was an argument I meant it. It was as though someone invented the method called square and then died before he could explain it. I am not saying that teachers cannot teach it, for they do. Nor am I saying they do not know what they are looking for, but I have asked many individuals to put it into words for me and they all have a different idea.

I attended a meeting with some twenty fellow teaching professionals, some of them recognized to be the top in the country. We were to set a simple formula for a method which we could allow school teachers to instruct to very young children prior to calling in a P.G.A. professional teacher. The lecturer, with a No. 7 iron in his hand said, "We start the club back like this. . . ."

Immediately four of my 'colleagues' stood up and said that as far as they were concerned the meeting was over for, they claimed, quite incorrectly, the the clubface, which had travelled a mere two feet, had turned open. We were halfway through the second day of that conference and we still had not got the clubhead beyond the two feet.

Further bad, or should I say incorrect, explanations given made clarification impossible, adding 'fuel' to the critics who opposed the method. The P.G.A. were accused of not getting a teaching method together, but how could they with members arguing, some too blind to see, others confused. If only they could all stand on a practice ground and watch the world's top twenty players they could do nothing but agree that the hands must hinge the wrists square to the left forearm, square to the plane of the swing.

I am not so blind that I insist that the hingeing of the wrists by the hands square to the plane is the only way that a golf ball may be hit well. What I am claiming is that this is the way that the young should be trained, this is the way that potential tournament players should be guided and anyone guiding such potential on a different course is hindering their progress. The physical ability of an individual has to be the determining factor, and a very high percentage of older people, lady golfers or people unable to turn the trunk of the body, would not be able to play with the square method. Any teacher who cannot accept that is an idiot. For such pupils a greater use of individual hand and wrist movement must be trained. But it must be accepted that this is a compromise! As a compromise it will enable everyone to play golf but if it involves movement outside the protection of the plane then it involves uncertainty.

a *Evolution* The design of early golf clubs promoted a rolling action of the hands and wrists. The extremely long and weighty head was capable of twisting the hickory shaft, the toe almost fanning, creating a torque in the shaft, first to the right and then to the left. This had to be timed and encouraged so that maximum value was gained at the strike.

The wrist action used when the top of the backswing was reached would be very much out of line with the player's left forearm. If one imagines that wrist joint frozen and the arm returned to its starting place the clubface would be many degrees turned outwards. This is why the cupped wrist shape at the top is known as open.

Incidentally the additional time required for the torque of the hickory shaft to unravel itself was gained by means of a lateral sway of the body. The sway gave more width to the arc, and with it time.

In later years the clubhead's length was reduced, taking away much of the torque. The central position began to take over from the sway and the excessive cupping of the wrists, which forced elbows to splay, was no longer necessary. The next stage is where the British, perhaps through tradition, missed out and refused to evolve. They accepted that with the loss of torque from the steel shaft the sway was no longer necessary, but they could not accept that the shorter, better-balanced clubhead did not need to be rolled open and the left wrist did not have to cup open from the line of its forearm. The position had evolved in the USA and was known as square. The hands were working, the wrists were hingeing but the clubface was remaining parallel to the line of the left forearm. It was simple, it was direct, why was it unacceptable? Fortunately, evolution cannot be stopped and the powers-that-were only delayed the inevitable.

I have illustrated Willie Park Junior, Open Champion of almost a hundred years ago, and Australian Bob Shearer at the top of their backswing; the only resemblance is in the moustache.

b *The Three Positions* I have illustrated three sets of hands at the top of a backswing, all having hinged the wrists to create the angle of leverage which is used to accelerate the clubhead through the base of its arc. They are known as:

1. SQUARE   2. OPEN   3. CLOSED

Whilst all of these positions could be arrived at with a twisting of a faulty grip, as explained in the chapter on grip, I am dealing with them only as having come from a correct start: good grip and correct alignment.

No. 1: square.   The hands have hinged the wrists and yet have preserved both themselves and the face of the club to the line of the back of the left forearm, as they were when they left the ball. They have been governed by the safety of the plane of the swing, and any hand action which can create sufficient leverage and yet live in the protection of plane must be consistent since the hinge which the hands create in the wrist joints shall not leave the direct line to the ball.

No. 2: open.   This is the most creative position. The hands can work independently of the plane of swing discarding its protection. Great amount of extra swing is made available, for the right elbow is no longer contained by the left side control. If this position was frozen and the arms returned to the set-up position the face of the club would be many degrees off to the right, in other words open. This shows the demand that is made with this action. The hands have to re-locate straight to hit the ball. They are doing a repair job on the downswing to square up the clubface.

No. 3: closed.   This position is found in most of the tournament players who set out to find square and overdo things. Trevino does it and sometimes Weiskopf does it, so it cannot be all bad. They prefer it going closed to going open. There is a safety device and that is the right arm which can only be pushed downwards so far, whereas in the open action the right arm is free to fly an unlimited amount. The pressure that closing the wrists pushes onto the right arm is used by some good players for additional thrust through the ball. There is a risk of causing back trouble using this method. If the position were frozen and the left arm returned to set-up position the clubface would be turned down, closed.

The only one of the three which could return to the set-up position and look like it could allow the player to hit the ball forward without adjustment is No. 1: square.

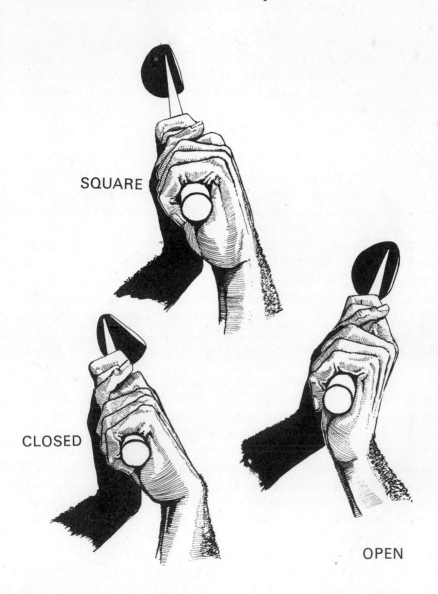

SQUARE

CLOSED

OPEN

c *Square to what?* The difficulty of explaining the hands hinge-ing the wrists square is encountered because of a lack of proper understanding of just what they are hingeing square to. Some misguided people actually thought that the clubface should swing square to the target, facing the target throughout the whole of the arc. This is a physical impossibility. However, early interpretations had golfers turning the clubface down-wards to start the backswing, believing that this would main-tain the wrist's hinge square also. This probably put many into hospital with disc trouble.

What do the hands hinge the wrists square to? *They hinge the wrists in such a manner that they not only develop leverage but allow the back of the left hand, the back of the left forearm and the face of the club to be square to the plane of the swing, the direct line of leverage to the ball.*

This all sounds too simple, but for a player to turn and to de-velop the power of a swing on plane he has to turn certain parts of him to his right, and that means open from the line to the target. This was the stumbling block, for just as the mis-interpreted versions of square frightened the establishment, the word open was like a red rag to a bull for the converted. However, the fact must be faced, on completion of the back-swing the following parts will have turned a full 90 degrees open from the line to the target in order that they may be square to the plane. The clubface. Back of left arm and hand. The shoul-ders.

Regardless of the fact that the clubface could turn 90 degrees immediately it does not, for that would be rolling open; it takes the same time to do its 90 degrees as the other departments. For it to turn open immediately there would have to be a turn of the wrist joint which would have made it open to the plane on arri-val at the top. The hinge that takes place between the back of the left arm and the hand is made from another source than rol-ling and this is where so many people missed the point. At the beginning of this book, on the subject of grip I pointed out that the left arm pointed out towards the direction of the ball and then to take up the grip the *fingers were turned to the ground. That arching forward and downward can also arch backward and upward. How much? Almost exactly 90 degrees. And that is the hinge that gives the leverage. That is the hinge which allows the back of the left hand, the back of the left forearm and the clubface to remain square to the plane.*

When does it get hinged? Over the whole of the backswing. It takes the same time to do its 90 degrees as the other components.

d *Open from what?*   When the hands hinge the wrists to the position known as open they turn the back of the left hand and the clubface away from the direct line of leverage and cause an argument with the plane of the swing. An early introduction of opening wrists to the backswing starts the clubface, hands and forearms off in an individual movement, detracting from the stability of correct shoulder turn.

I have deliberately drawn only three images of the player as against four on the previous page because the hand movement not being tuned to the shoulder movement can get the club to the top in a snatching action, a fault very common in this method of swinging.

Another point shown in the drawing as opposed to the one on square is that the club shaft makes two distinct directional moves. The early wrist action drives the club behind the player. Then with instinct searching for the direct line of leverage the shaft suddenly turns upwards vertically, cupping the wrists into an even weaker position. Now what goes up two ways has got to come down two ways, hasn't it?

The lack of balanced co-ordination in an early open take-away from the ball causes a confusion as to what direction the club should leave the ball. This does not happen when the clubhead, the hands, the arms, and the shoulders come away together. The clubhead must travel back slightly inwards since that is where correct plane is to be found, and correct plane will dictate the amount.

Any reader who is not convinced that swinging square and in plane is the best way has only to reverse the drawings and imagine just how dangerous a downswing with all the changes of direction must be.

e *A mechanical explanation* Of the three positions I have shown of the hands hingeing the wrists, only two are actually taught. Square and open. Closed is never taught, it is a position which many great players use but it is basically their version of square overdone to suit their particular requirements. A beginner would create very bad movement attempting to find it.

I have drawn two very mechanical top-of-the-backswing positions showing why square, the top drawing, is preferred by players who are continually under pressure. It is clearly seen by use of wooden blocks around the left arm and the shaft of the club just how the wrist joint is hinged a full 90 degrees without interfering with the plane of the swing. The back of the left arm, the back of the left hand, and the face of the club are all absolutely true to the direct line of greatest leverage to the ball.

The bottom drawing shows what square believers feel is the danger of open wrist and clubface swinging. They believe that as the left hand and clubface turn open from the plane they tear away from the protection of the plane and a repair job will be necessary to get the clubface back to its alignment position at impact.

The advantage of the open action, if one ignores the screws coming loose, is that a greater angle of leverage is created between left arm and the shaft, more than 90 degrees. Should a person be physically incapable of a full body turn or of strong leg work then that extra leverage will be necessary to them. It creates more risk, for the screws will have to be replaced in time to hit the ball. Not before, or the clubface will pass through too soon, causing an early hit. Not too late or the clubface will be left trailing, open to the target.

6 HIPS, LEGS AND FEET

The initial introduction of movement to the hips, legs and feet is made as the player swings off in search of plane. It is caused by the pressure of the weight of the arc moving and turning from the front to the right and behind the player. The body's weight, originally shared evenly between the feet, must be moving from the left in favour of the right side and should be allowed, by means of the left knee flexing and the break of the left ankle, to take the left heel from the ground.

A beginner should never feel that there is safety in keeping his left heel solidly down. In an elementary swing when the right hip gathers the pressure, the right leg will be straightening and with the left becoming shorter because of bending joints, a loss of height and balance would occur if the heel did not rise. In fact keeping the left heel fastened to the ground straightens the leg, causing the pressure of the swing to pull the body weight over to the player's right and promotes a lateral sway.

The correct hip, leg and footwork to the backswing movements are more allowed to happen rather than made to happen, for they must be brought about by the swinging arc. If they are forced to happen without the pull of the swing they would undermine the swing's power. The hips would be turning as full as the shoulders, creating a turn which has no wind and a backswing must be a wound-up movement or it has no leverage.

The top of the backswing is built up on the principle of a spiral. It is wound from the straight line of the target line on which the feet are placed, gathering degrees of turn as it progresses upwards through the knees, the hips, on through the trunk to the final 90 degrees of the fully turned shoulders.

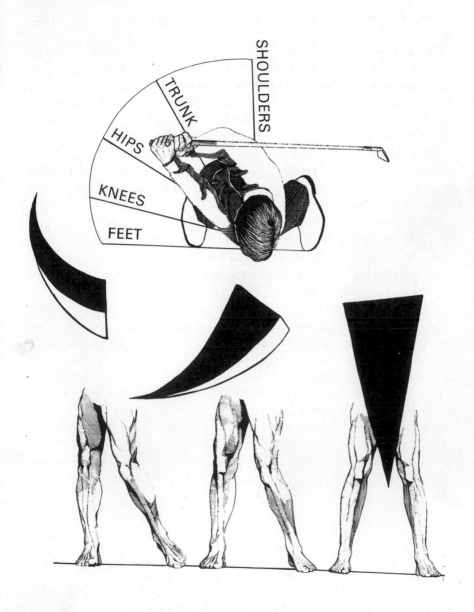

Incorrect Movement. Correct hip movement is essential to good swinging but like so many parts of a golf swing it has to be encompassed in the general overall mental picture of the swing. For it to be thought of as outside this overall picture is to invite danger. The hips do not initiate the backswing, they must be drawn into it.

To commence a backswing from hip action without the invitation from the upward wind of the swing into plane must turn the hips too soon and too much. The right hip will be pushed backwards until the hip socket virtually jams and there it will stay until the swinging arc is well on its way back to the ball. This will detract from the correct preparation which is intended to offer the left hip as a puller. As well as jamming the right hip socket this premature movement will drive the right knee back and will brace the leg, immobilizing it from enjoying a free follow through.

Another very common incorrect hip movement is used when the player moves the right hip away in a lateral direction. This also serves to immobilize the shoulder turn.

Unfortunately, the early introduction of hip movement is not the only cause which drives the right hip backwards so that it jams. Players who swing the club back from the ball, turning the wrists and clubface open, turn the arc behind them so soon that the right leg is forced straight, driving the hip socket back so that it jams again. Fortunately, as much as 'bad plane' swinging can destroy good hip turn, 'good plane' can make it. The type of swing a player employs dictates the movement required from the bottom half.

The right hip is there to gather the pressure of the turn, not to make it!

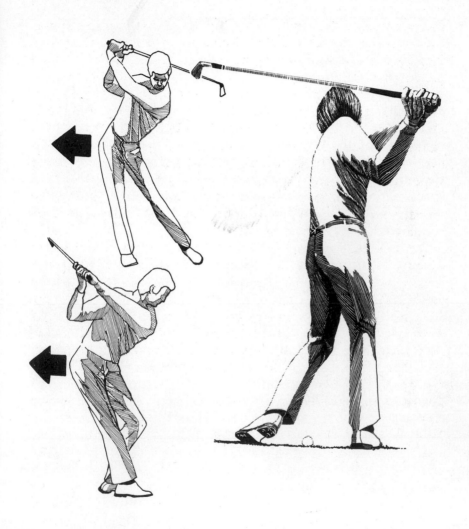

10

Downswing

1 HAND AND WRIST ACTION

From open. The player who uses the wrist action known as open to reach the top of his backswing is very likely to be out of plane, not in direct line of leverage, and is going to have to create a lot of hand and wrist work to both find the line and the target, giving an impression of great clubhead speed. This speed is only the excessive movement created in a short space and nowhere near matches the value of the wrists undoing solidly in a direct line approach.

There is a great sense of timing required for a wrist-flicking action and under pressure this is not easily found. The wrists hinged in plane are not probing for the ball, and may give more value in their simpler role.

From 'square'. From the top of the backswing, with the line direct, the hands and arms pull the shaft down through the ball. The wrists have a 90 degree hinge to dispose of and centrifugal throw is all too willing to get rid of that. Many great players consciously add a feeling of solidness to the wrists through the strike to avoid even that throw being too active.

John O'Leary, a charming young Irishman, is a perfect example of solid, square in-plane swinging. In fact he is a living proof of what I am writing. He used to be an open, wristy player. He studied under a top American teacher for one month and the whole time was spent making him solid, simple and square. His whole attitude to hitting a ball is "to make as little happen in the wrists going from the ball then back through it, the only movement created by leverage and momentum". Watching him hit the ball one wonders why he hits it so far doing what appears to be so little, when others flay about creating nothing any longer, only more trouble.

I have illustrated John on his way to impact. This is the point where he stays 'positive'. He can afford to stay that way: he has come from such a direct line that he does not have to find anything.

In the top inset, this is how John now comes through. In the bottom his wrists fold as they used to when too much went on through the strike. I officiated in a match at Laurel Valley

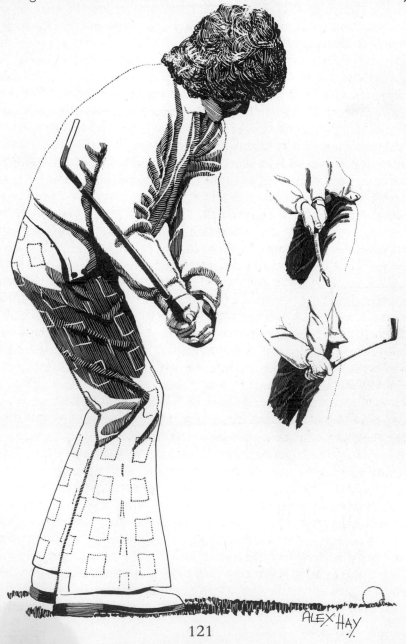

when John played against Hale Irwin, both students of the same method. The pair were so consistent it almost became boring, just a couple of little putts at the end deciding the contest for Irwin.

2 EDUCATED HANDS

I have shown in this chapter that the hands should only hinge the wrists into open if the player physically needs the assistance of extra flexibility because of the risk involved. I could be accused of discouraging the 'education of the hands' but that is not my intention. A player who is physically capable should hinge square, but he should also know how to use open, for that is from where he may deliberately manoeuvre twist into a ball's flight. It is, after all, a position which has to have adjustment and what makes it vulnerable also makes it adaptable.

It is not difficult to educate the hands and wrists in to the open process, but before it is used on a long club it should be learned with a short one such as a pitching club.

For example, I have claimed that certain departments turn 90 degrees, shoulders, arms and hands, the wrists matching with a 90 degrees hinge, all contributing to a FULL square-to-plane swing. When the spinal posture comes over to the shorter club a 90 degree turn of the body is almost impossible. This is accepted and the rest of the departments would lose the equivalent amount, that is if the swing were to remain square. But if the arms, the hands and the wrists pushed on for their full quota the swing plane would lift upwards and left wrist would cup open. (The very principle on which lack of shoulder turn makes slice in a full shot.)

Therefore, in a smaller stroke of some 40–50 yards, with the feet close together and by deliberately cutting the shoulder turn, the wrist hinge would have to be in excess and the back of the left hand and the clubface would open, the shaft of the club climbing steeply out of the protection of the plane. Greater backspin will be imparted but great care must be taken to see that this extra hand and wrist action takes the club up more steeply and never more flat. Prolonged practice of this should be discouraged, for it will damage the full swing by its promotion of individual movement.

One great player who lives with the fact that he has to make extra hand action is Peter Oosterhuis. He does not get sufficient shoulder turn, it is halved by an almost non-existent hip

turn in the backswing, brought about by his particular physique. Peter knows this and 'works' the ball very successfully
with his hand and wrist action. Every now and then the lack of
turn tells, and one gets away. It is strange how a couple of bad
shots seen on television 'write off' the tremendous perform-
ances. Thank God, Peter accepts the odd one, he is a great com-
petitor who has to use his hands.

3 HANDS AND ARMS, HIPS, LEGS AND FEET

When the completed backswing arc is ready to commence the downswing to and through the ball it needs the co-operation of the hips, legs and feet. The preparation, even that of an elementary hip, leg and footwork is sufficient to give the required movement. All of the build-up of a correctly planed backswing is geared for a downward pull, and the left hip, leg and foot are pullers.

The left hip which has turned towards the front is willing to pull back past its original place. The left knee which has kinked inwards is willing to pull back to where it came from and the left foot and ankle, hingeing from ball of foot and ankle joint are more than willing to pull their opposite too.

Many teachers of golf use the lower half of the body to ignite the downswing and whilst it may be debatable whether this starts the downswing or not it certainly does no harm. Personally I feel that it is perfectly safe to co-ordinate the top half with the bottom provided the 'pullers' of that area only are used, the under-the-shoulder muscles of the left side, the under muscles of the left arm and the back muscles of the hands. In this way all that is designed to be pulled pulls through.

The transfer of weight caused by pulling through takes the load of the movement into the left hip, leg and foot and the counterparts on the right are given almost complete freedom to follow the flow of the arc, the momentum of the arc carrying the right foot entirely up onto its toes.

The difference in the left-foot performance in the backswing to the right foot in the through swing is created because of the fact that the backswing is a preparation, the through swing is a release. The left foot is flexed for action to come, under the control of precision. The right has the joy of flowing on through in free pursuit of the arc.

The angle created in my top drawing shows a player arriving at the top of his backswing. He is correctly in plane and he is ready to start the downswing. If he happened to be a top tournament player he would, at this point be moving quite fluidly and this leads me to the question of starting down with 'ALL THE PULLERS' or starting down with the left-hip pulling.

To the expert the upward momentum of the clubhead could still be working when the left hip starts back towards the target and this may cause the angle between the left forearm and the shaft to become very acute, as in the lower drawing. The leverage of the up-moving club weight on to the wrists as the left hip tugs back brings the shaft closer to the forearm than at any point in the swing. This acute angle to the expert means more acceleration through the ball and to some it becomes worth the risk involved.

To the weekend player or to the higher-handicap player it could well create an angle which he would be unable to get rid of in time to strike the ball square. This is known as a late hit. For him consciously to lead with his left hip he would no doubt be mentally neglecting his hands and this would lead to push shots to the right of the target.

The benefit of the swing being square to the plane is shown in these two drawings, for although the angle is increasing in the lower one the blade of the club retains the same parallel line to that of the forearm. I would recommend that average golfers should settle for the top position and feel all of the pullers pull together and leave the left hip leading to the better players. The angle created in the top drawing is very adequate indeed.

Johnny Miller is a player who swings his club up 'open' from the plane. He is also one of the experts at leading the downswing with a very obvious left-hip pull. He uses this hip movement to pull tight any 'loose strings' his backswing might have caused and at this point he becomes a typical American square-to-the-plane swinger.

It would be most upsetting if the square-to-the-plane swing gave anyone the impression that the hands do not hit the ball, for that is not the case. They can hit it just as firmly as the player is capable of doing. All that is suggested by the method is that there shall be no individual flashing of the wrists which make it look as though a lot is going on when often very little is happening.

There is a greater attachment to the feet and legs with a square swing, in fact, a greater attachment to all of the other departments. Working on a direct path gives the look of solidness, and the greater simplicity gives a false illusion of non-violence in some cases. But one should remember that players like Palmer, Player, Jacklin and many others use the method and it is an advantage to their power. Then it is shown working more gracefully with Littler, Irwin and others. How can it be wrong?

I have drawn the hands, wrists and clubhead coming through the strike from a square-to-the-plane position showing the legs helping. Not help as in panic, but help as in co-ordination. The hands hitting through as a pair. None of this rubbish about one hand hitting past the other!

From the open-to-the-plane position the club would be travelling in from a flatter angle because the hands started their first movement vertically downwards before they tried to find the correct track to the ball. In this case the legs would not be assisting but creating a barrier so that the right hand may snap over the left.

It is acknowledged that the impact area requires a resistance, in the same way that a man with a hammer would create very little, if his forearm continued in lead of the wrist and hammer head. It is only when his forearm's downward movement meets resistance that impact value is attained.

In the square swing the resistance comes from the player maintaining position. For although his hips and legs go on through there is left an invisible barrier, this is the line from the head to the ground remaining immediately above the spot over which it started.

11

Through Swings

1 HIPS, LEGS AND FEET

Much has been written lately of using the leg action in a creative capacity, exaggerating its role out of all proportion. It is the shape of the swing technique, the type of hand and wrist action, and the angle of the plane which decide the movement of the legs through the swing. There has to be learned a basic common sense transfer of pressure from foot to foot, leg to leg, and hip to hip to allow the swinging arc the benefit of weight transfer and good width. After that whether the knees are bent or straight depends entirely on the method being used to swing the club.

A club swung to the pattern I have described as square will be travelling that way through to the target quite a long way after the impact and will want the legs out of the way, they must not create any barrier.

A swing to the pattern described as open requires a barrier to hit past to enable the clubface to snap from being open to straight. The barrier is a firm left side and a firm left leg.

A problem was created in the early days of square swinging when the new type of hand and wrist action was matched up to the leg action suited to the requirements of the open swing. The clubhead was unable to pass the barrier and the ball was pushed away.

The handwork and the legwork must match. Square-to-the-plane swinging must have the legs flexed through the ball. Open-to-the-plane must have a firm left leg to hit past.

When correct matching legwork is found through the ball it is almost certain that preparation for what is to happen will show in the legs during the backswing. The right leg of the square-to-plane swinger will remain in a flexed shape whilst the open-to-plane swinger will tend to drive his back straight. Both are correct if matched to the rest of the swing.

I have illustrated two players just after impact. The one on the left is coming from a square position with his legs remaining flexed to enable the clubface to drive on unimpeded. The one on the right has come to the strike with the clubface open and has used the braced left leg to hit past and straighten up the blade of the club.

Good through swinging is the result of what has gone before coupled with the ambition of what is to come. What has gone is grip, ball position, posture, plane, hip, leg and footwork. And when they have all got the player to the top of the backswing, with the direct line of leverage asserted the through swing is well on its way.

The ambition of what is to come is the follow-through, the proof that all that has gone before has been correctly done. Nothing must impede the flow of the swing. When all the built up leverage passes the base of its arc the lever is spent, the ball is on its way and the swing is releasing on through.

2   EARLY AND LATE HITTING

One might think that after the leverage is used there can be no need to worry since the ball has gone, but that is not so. Any neglect of completion of the arc will start an infection which will eat back through the arc until it takes effect where damage can be done. If all the built-up leverage is not given consistent guidance as to the correct path after the strike it will release itself in an inconsistent pattern. This is commonly described as early and late hitting.

A player must have a solid positive feel well through the ball, rather like a sprinter who is still travelling as fast after 110 yards when the tape was already broken at 100 yards. No deterioration must be allowed to filter back and weaken the purpose. Tony Jacklin, especially when under pressure is one of the game's longest drivers, and this comes from the tremendous width his arc maintains through and on after the ball.

The great danger of a player passing his right hand over his left is that the LEFT ELBOW gets information contrary to 'wide through the ball' and it begins to buckle, throwing the elbows apart. The continuity of width between the elbows throughout the swing is essential to smooth swinging.

ALEX HAY

12

The Follow-through

All that remains is the follow-through, the quality of which proves that balance, timing, and quality of swing have gone before. This is the position which all players should establish so that it becomes in their minds the 'finish of the swing'. This gets them away from any idea that the ball is the end product. The drawing shows how the position of the head is maintained to the finish without it interfering with the process of the arc.

The expression 'head-down' used to be of great importance to the golf swing prior to the evolution of the square-to-the-plane swing. The open action which required a braced left side to be hit up against encouraged the player's head to stay glued looking at the turf long after the strike. But that same head down would impede the wide flow of the modern swing.

Of course the eyes have to be on the ball at impact, they can even remain behind for an instant, but the head should be allowed to turn so that the player's face may follow the flow of the swing. The only responsibility of the head is that it maintains a constant position above the spot over which it started, and by doing so preserves the spinal tilt which existed at the set-up, and at the top of the backswing, right through to completion, so that the arc remains safe within the protection of its plane to completion.

The more simple through-the-ball square-to-plane action with the flexed left side, which the correct plane has encouraged, has no need for the neck muscles to jam so that the head can remain rigidly looking down whilst the player's partner looks for the ball. If the head jams the swing must either stop or the wrists must fold. This makes a tremendous wrench on the left elbow joint and is no way to promote a true flight on the ball.

The Follow-through

All the work has been done. The follow-through is the result and is to be enjoyed. The player, particularly if he is a beginner, should make great efforts to hold the follow-through position for several seconds. Not only does the poise have a look of quality, and style is important, but it stops any bad habits creeping back. It is like tying a knot in a piece of string. If you do not the frayed end will creep farther and farther back until it is of no use.